Years of wisdom and real-life experiences are captured in the answers in *Ask a Missionary*. I highly recommend this book for anyone, any age, considering a mission-related ministry.

DON PARROTT
President, Finishers Project/MissionNext

John McVay has more passion than anyone I know for mobilizing people to become effective missionaries. This book combines his passion with the expertise and practical advice of over one hundred missionaries.

JOHN CROUCH, MD
President, In His Image International

Want real advice from real people who've been there and know how best to answer what you are asking? This book has it. I will use *Ask a Missionary* as a reference to help me—and many others—for years to come.

SCOTT MOREAU
Professor, Wheaton College
Editor, *Evangelical Missions Quarterly*

This book is like having a dozen missionary friends at your side, coaching you with kindness and clarity. Who knew wisdom could be so encouraging?

STEVE HAWTHORNE
Co-editor, *Perspectives on the World Christian Movement*

Ask a Missionary is strategic, relevant, and a powerful tool for those thinking about becoming a missionary.

GEORGE VERWER
Founder, Operation Mobilization

D0830330

This book is a great resource for mission mobilizers, pastors, Christian leaders, and anyone coaching those exploring missionary service.

MARTI SMITH
Mission mobilizer, Caleb Resources

Many express interest in cross-cultural ministry; yet, few actually go. This book is packed with helpful tips and insights to make sure you don't get lost on the journey toward mission involvement.

RYAN SHAW
International lead facilitator, Student Volunteer Movement 2

People fear what they don't understand. This resource answers the questions most commonly asked by prospective and current missionaries alike. I would love to put this into the hands of every university student we meet.

CLAUDE HICKMAN
Executive director, The Traveling Team

John McVay has compiled this wonderful collection of wisdom to help prospective missionaries get to the field. I wish this book had been available when we first launched into missions.

JUSTIN LONG
Senior editor, The Network for Strategic Missions

There could be no better primer for cross-cultural ministry than the practical, cogent advice presented in this book by seasoned missionaries.

DAVID SHIBLEY
President, Global Advance

Ask a Missionary gives concise and practical insight for those pursuing missionary service.

LARRY WALKER
Regional director, Advancing Churches in Missions Commitment (ACMC)

The questions in *Ask a Missionary* are the ones being asked by my students. The answers given are superb. I'm going to require my students to read this book.

HOWARD CULBERTSON
Professor, Southern Nazarene University

The path to missionary service is poorly marked. Those who have gone before could be of great help, if you could know their answers to your questions. With *Ask a Missionary,* now you can.

DAVID MAYS
Director of learning initiatives, The Mission Exchange

Ask a Missionary

Ask a Missionary

Time-Tested Answers from Those Who've Been There

JOHN MCVAY, GENERAL EDITOR

Authentic

Authentic Publishing
A Ministry of Biblica
We welcome your questions and comments.

USA	1820 Jet Stream Drive, Colorado Springs, CO 80921
	www.authenticbooks.com
India	Logos Bhavan, Medchal Road, Jeedimetla Village, Secunderabad
	500 055, A.P.

Ask a Missionary
ISBN-13: 978-1-93406-887-8

Printed in the United States of America

Library of Congress Catalog: McVay, John
Ask a Missionary: Time-Tested Answers from Those Who've Been There
A catalog record for this book is available through the Library of Congress.

CONTENTS

CONTRIBUTORS

ELISABETH ELLIOT

Elisabeth and her husband Jim Elliot helped translate the New Testament into the language of the Quichua Indians in Ecuador. Later, Auca Indians killed Jim as he attempted to take the gospel to that primitive tribe. Elisabeth continued her work with the Quichuas and later lived and worked among the Aucas. She is author of *Through Gates of Splendor* and other books.

STEVE HOKE

Steve Hoke served as professor of missions and director of campus ministries at Seattle Pacific University, director of field training for World Vision International, and president of LIFE Ministries (Japan). Currently he is vice president of people development for Church Resource Ministries. Steve is coauthor of *Global Mission Handbook*.

MARK HUDDLESTON

Mark worked as a missionary with Pioneer Bible Translators in Zaire. He is now a professor at Nebraska Christian College, where he teaches missions, languages, and church growth.

PHYLLIS KILBOURN

Phyllis Kilbourn is a missionary with WEC International and founder of Rainbows of Hope, a holistic ministry to children in crisis. She is president of Crisis Care Training International and author of numerous books, including *Healing the Children of War* and *Sexually Exploited Children:Working to Protect and Heal*.

JOHN MCVAY

John McVay served as a missions pastor in Tulsa and coordinated ten Heartland MissionsFest conferences. Then he and his family served in France for a year with WEC. Since 1998, John has been administrator for In His Image International Medical Missions. He also helped launch AskAMissionary.com and The Journey Deepens retreats.

DON PARROTT

Don Parrott worked as a missions pastor in the Pacific Northwest. Then he and his family served as missionaries with OC International in Argentina. Don was leader of Paraclete Mission Group for several years and is now president of Finishers Project, which connects adults with mission opportunities.

NEAL PIROLO

Neal Pirolo directed a ministry school in San Diego for five years and then developed a prefield training course that has been modeled internationally. Neal's first book, *Serving As Senders*, is available in twenty languages. He also wrote *I Think God Wants Me to Be a Missionary: Issues to Deal with Long before You Say Goodbye.*

JIM RAYMO

Jim Raymo worked for seventeen years with WEC International, training mission candidates and later as the U.S. director. He now teaches at Bethany College of Missions and Northwestern College. Jim is author of *Marching to a Different Drummer: Rediscovering Missions in an Age of Affluence and Self-Interest.*

BILL STEARNS

William (Bill) Stearns and his wife, Amy, wrote a number of books, including *Catch the Vision 2000, Run with the Vision,* and *2020 Vision.* They worked in France for five years as part of a church-planting effort and a marketplace-mission business. They served with Finishers Project and MissionNext, coaching midcareer adults into missions.

DAVID STEVENS

David Stevens, a family physician, served as executive officer and medical missionary at Tenwek Hospital in Kenya. Later, as medical director of Samaritan's Purse, he led an emergency medical team to Somalia in the midst of war. David wrote the book *Jesus M.D.* and is CEO of the Christian Medical and Dental Associations.

JACK VOELKEL

Jack Voelkel is a missionary who served with Latin America Mission in Peru and Colombia, first as a student worker and then as a professor in the Biblical Seminary in Medellin. Since 2000, Jack has served as Urbana's missionary-in-residence and answers questions in the Ask Jack column of Urbana.org.

ONE HUNDRED OTHER MISSIONARIES

Over ten years, missionaries from around the world contributed answers through AskAMissionary.com to questions asked by people exploring some aspect of mission work.

IMAGINE
Your Own Gripping Story

1

WELCOME.

Yes, we are missionaries—more than one hundred of us—ready to take your questions. Actually, some of us have been hanging around here for almost a decade waiting for you. Whether you're a short-term mission fan or you're exploring lifelong missionary service—and regardless of your age or station in life—relax. Take a seat and get a good cup of something global. How about java? Coke? Kimchi, with its fermented, spicy-cabbage flavor? Koumiss, made from mare's milk?

We'll offer some hardcore biblical responses to your ask-a-missionary questions. We are committed to sharing our insights about serving in the most wonderful, challenging, grand, irritating, spiritual, eternity-impacting endeavor in the world: missions.

THE SEARCH FOR ANSWERS

Throughout this book, we'll explore the aspects of missionary service you rarely get to discuss with those who've been there. Face it. If you were aspiring to become a firefighter, you could easily wander downtown to your local fire station and talk over the occupation with firefighters. If you were thinking about a health-care role, you could talk to a nurse or doctor who attends your church. But there are few opportunities to talk over missionary life with real missionaries. That's why we're getting together—so you can ask a missionary.

We'll cover five categories of questions: guidance; agencies; training; funding; and singles, couples, and kids. In some of the chapters, you'll sense that virtually every question applies to you personally. In other chapters some questions will apply more to your fellow seekers. And for some questions we'll offer a range of answers: *yes, no, maybe, no, yes, perhaps.* Regardless, these insights, contributed by those who've completed their own discovery process, will make a huge difference in helping you better understand missionary service.

Each chapter opens with a story of God's actual work in some part of his globe. Names, location, and some details are altered, since much of what God is doing in the world occurs in areas where proclaiming the gospel is illegal or dangerous. But the core of each story—the events, the individuals, the miracles, the impact—is real, as real as the experiences that will characterize your life if you become a missionary.

Each chapter ends with introspective questions, found in the section "My Thoughts So Far." Consider carefully these next-step questions. When combined with prayer and the Holy Spirit's guidance, they will launch your exploration of God's plan for you in missions. Journal your answers, and then discuss your responses with a leader or friend from your local church.

How do we know God will guide you? Because he promises to guide—when we take time to ask and listen: "*Ask* and it will be given to you; *seek* and you will find; *knock* and the door will be opened to you. For everyone who asks *receives*; he who seeks *finds*; and to him who knocks, *the door will be opened*" (Matthew 7:7–8, emphasis added).

TOWARD YOUR OWN STORY

Most Christians today meander through very normal life-styles. They digest Bible teaching and enjoy fellowship at their local church. They love Jesus, go to lots of meetings, and wait for heaven.

But when you commit yourself to ministry through missions in God's global purpose, when you submit to the advance of his kingdom, your life becomes anything but normal. You can join God in beating against the gates of hell to free some from every people, tribe, tongue, and nation.

Imagine being single in the stark reaches of the mountains of China. And there, opening an Italian restaurant that attracts travelers who rave about the eggplant Parmesan, lasagna, brick-oven pizza, and desserts such as tiramisu. Imagine requiring your fifteen local restaurant workers to attend in-house Bible classes—at which one soul after the other comes to faith in Jesus Christ.

Imagine being the one in Manila to introduce a homosexual bartender to Christ. And he, with your coaching, shares the gospel with the sixty-five prostitutes he supervises as a pimp. All find Jesus, meet together in the bar for Bible studies, and eventually form a church. Imagine the former-pimp-led fellowship reproducing ten new cell groups in the neighborhood.

Imagine being the Christian foreigner working among the drought-plagued coffee plantations of Uganda. And there, convincing thirty-four non-Christian coffee growers to pray for rain *in the name of Jesus*. Imagine the heavens suddenly breaking and the sky pouring rain. The Ugandan farmers come to faith in Christ.

Imagine being a missionary who trains new missionaries in

Costa Rica. And some churches there—for the first time in their histories—sending out their own missionaries. Imagine sixty of your missionary trainees going to the uttermost parts of the earth.

These missionary stories, and thousands of others like them, won't make the headline news, at least not until we, in heaven, share all God has done in us and through us. Yet right now the world is being changed by thousands and thousands of missionaries—and you could become one of them, with your own cross-cultural ministry as gripping as those of the missionaries you'll meet in each chapter.

Jesus invites each of us to participate in his global mission. He invites us to join him—somewhere, in some way—in making disciples among the unreached. So let's jump into the next chapter to begin exploring ways God may lead us in his great mission story.

GUIDANCE
Discovering God's Plan

2

IT WAS SUNDOWN IN HARBIN, THE SMOKY CAPITAL of Heilongjiang Province in far northern China. Waiting in the evening drizzle for the last train, the only thing that moved was the cold shiver down my spine. Back at the hotel, my short-term exploration team was settling in for their nightly dinner together.[*]

We were in China to explore the possibility of working there as Christian missionaries. But that afternoon I had taken a sightseeing tour across the city. A Mandarin-speaking guide and I wandered through the Russian-style Church of St. Sophia. And in one of my more brave moments, I tasted a street vendor's soup, which the guide had declared to be "donkey-dumpling stew." A bit unsettling, but tasty.

Suddenly realizing I had no idea when the last evening train departed, I rushed back to the station. As I fidgeted on the bench alongside the tracks, certain I'd missed the train, one of those undeniable God moments happened. You know, a "chance meeting" when you clearly recognize that the Creator of the universe just stamped a divine "Yes!" on your prayer list—right next to the question, "God, do you want me to be a missionary?"

---

[*]   Each chapter in this book begins with a fictionalized version of a true story, edited by Bill Stearns. The names, location, and some details are altered, since much of God's work today occurs in areas where proclaiming the gospel is illegal or dangerous.

It started when a young couple rolled their American-made road bikes next to me at the station.

"Sorry. Do you speak English?"

"Yes. Yes I do!" came my startled reply.

"We don't usually see tourists in this part of the city," the man said, holding out his hand. "Justin. And my wife Terra. And you are . . . ?"

I introduced myself and with relief rattled out my confusion on the train schedule, that I needed to get back to my team, and my reason for being in China. With a kindly nod, Terra gestured at the approaching train. "Sit with us?"

On the commuter run back across Harbin, Justin told me their story.

"We flew here two years ago from Canada—a fourteen-hour flight with our two toddlers. Not a good time to be told by the customs agent that our road bikes required an import duty of two thousand U.S. dollars! We were exhausted and really frustrated, so we just said goodbye to the bikes. The four of us squashed into a taxi for the ride to the apartment Terra's international school had arranged for us. She was going to teach English there; I was going to be Mr. Mom."

Terra jumped into the story. "Three days later, I got a call from the airport about our bikes. I tried to understand the official, who thankfully threw in some English here and there. I carefully told him in Mandarin, 'Of course, we'd love to have the bicycles. The international school begins tomorrow! . . . No, we cannot pay two thousand dollars U.S. . . . Yes, I'm an English teacher. . . . What?

You'll bring the bikes to the school tomorrow?'

"So the next day, a truck drove up with both our bikes. A man in a business suit climbed out of the cab's passenger side and told Justin and me, 'Now, you will do something for me!'"

Dim overhead lights kicked on inside our train car—just as Justin joked, "Shades of the mafia or something!" We all laughed.

Justin continued, "The airport official said to Terra, 'I have done you a great favor, and now you must teach English in my school for airline staff.' Terra argued, saying, 'But how can I, our home is hours away from the airport, and I teach all day?' With no hesitation, the man said. 'My training school is in your part of the city.'

"Then he looked at me, and I muttered in my less-than-fluent Mandarin, 'I stay home with the children during the day.' Once again he insisted, 'I want you to teach only in the evenings.'

"Well, that was two years ago, and every time we tell this story we're amazed all over again at how God arranged for us to work exactly where he wanted us. But the story gets better," Justin said. "I'm not an English teacher. But my wife had brought to China some basic English-learning lessons—which I used to teach the airline staff. And, my job in Canada? Working as a flight attendant, of course. So I felt right at home with my new airline students. I even drafted a training manual for the school, which the official appreciated."

Then, as if Justin and Terra could see that divine "Yes!" stamp as clearly as I could, they began unfolding my first lessons on living as a witness of Jesus Christ in China.

"One night, while riding my bike home from teaching a class," Justin began, "a young man pedaled hard to catch up with me, just to rave about my road bike. Speaking English, he invited me to cycle with him the following Saturday in the countryside, and I accepted. During that ride, he said he was open to studying Scripture with me, and within a few weeks, he received Christ as his Savior."

Terra gave the next lesson. "About that time, many of the airline students made our apartment their hangout, mostly out of curiosity and to practice English. After a month or so, we asked if they'd like to learn about the Bible. That's how a Bible study group was born in our front room! We eventually had dozens of new friends. We cooked meals together and rode scooters to the mountains—singing praise songs with a boom box in the town squares along the way. We studied the Scriptures together, and every week several students committed their lives to Christ.

"After six months or so, some of the airline staffers moved to other cities—and started Bible studies of their own. One even enrolled in a formal Bible school and is now a full-time missionary . . . in Tibet!"

In the dark, the commuter train slowed to a stop and the doors clunked open. I followed the couple as they rolled their bikes onto the shadowy platform. Then, as if they recognized our "chance meeting" was nearly over, Justin and Terra, one after the other, downloaded two years worth of wisdom for my taking.

"Practice hospitality, even if you're in a small apartment. Invite everybody and anybody over. Provide outlines at the Bible studies; these new believers will multiply the studies with others! Ask for prayer needs, and pray for miracles. Have a stash of Bible-reference books and discs as a lending library.

"Make friends all over the community—in the bank, the

market, the post office, the park. People love to practice English, so you have an immediate inroad to friendship. Ride bikes in order to chat with other riders and then invite them to the church in your home. Relationships couldn't have been built if we were the usual foreigners in a tinted-window car.

"Celebrate all the Christian holidays. Remember that as a follower of Christ, everything you do—your hobby, sports, handcrafts, music—is a bridge to introduce someone to Christ."

They finally caught their collective breath, and I asked, somewhat hopefully, if they were in China permanently. Terra looked down. "Tonight is our final fun-ride downtown. Tomorrow we leave, back to Canada."

Although I hated for this divine encounter to end, I knew I had something big to tell the team back at the hotel. So Justin and I exchanged e-mail addresses, and we parted as if old friends.

I received this e-mail from Justin and Terra not long ago.

> A few days into the new year, we heard from the one least likely to make it in her new faith. She's started a number of Bible study groups and, just before Christmas, led thirty members to the Lord—at one time! Another has attended Bible school in the United States and is now preparing to be a tentmaking missionary to the Arab world. God continues to work through the small group we left behind.

I'm thankful for God's perfect guidance to me that night, and I can't wait for my own China story to begin.

SIGNS OF DIVINE DIRECTION

Like Justin and Terra, you'll probably learn fast that God doesn't always unfold his plans according to our missionary-life expectations.

> "The mind of *man plans his way*,
> but *the LORD directs his steps*."
> (Proverbs 16:9, emphasis added)

The apostle Paul, throughout the book of Acts, modeled flexibility as he faced unexpected opportunities and challenges. As we take our first steps in discovering God's guidance, let's also remain flexible. For God may divert our steps toward an unexpected—and amazing—plan!

So how does he guide us? Let's think and pray through these signs of divine direction.[†]

Q. How can I know if God is leading me to become a missionary?

[†] John McVay has gathered and edited questions and answers for this book for over ten years through the website AskAMissionary.com. Each missionary's experience and agency affiliation were current when the answer was written. In most cases, the missionary's last name is omitted for security reasons.

A. Look for an inner conviction, for godly counsel, and then for an agency.

Three Cs are vital to knowing and following God's will:

- **Conviction**. This comes from studying the Bible, praying, hearing sermons, reading mission material, and focusing on God's plan for the world and your part in fulfilling it.
- **Counsel**. Share your thoughts with godly leaders and friends to receive prayer and suggestions.
- **Circumstances**. Contact a mission agency, go on a short-term exposure trip, and talk to missionaries. Keep marching ahead as doors continue to open.

One caution: don't mix the order above. That is, don't look at circumstances before the inner conviction and before godly counsel.

Answer from Merle, who served for twenty-one years in Ethiopia and Sudan with Serving in Mission (SIM).

A. Stay close to God and trust him to lead in unmistakable ways.

When our sons were about three years old and just learning to express themselves in English, we spent countless hours trying to figure out what they wanted or what they were trying to tell us. In contrast, when I was a teenager and my father wanted the grass mowed before he came home from work, he never had a problem getting his expectations across to me. Now, I could have turned to my older brother and said, "You know, I think Dad may want me to mow the grass today, but I'm just not sure. How can I be certain of Dad's will on this matter?" But of course my brother would have thought I had gone nuts to ask such a thing.

Is our heavenly Father, the Creator of heaven and earth, any less able than my earthly dad to communicate his will in clear and unmistakable terms? I think not. If you have to puzzle over a feeling or seek help in interpreting a sign, then it most likely is not direction from God.

Those of us raised in the church learned *about* God while we were young. Unfortunately, we often fail to *know* God. We must nurture a personal relationship with the Father in order to hear his voice or even to understand the proper context of that which we do hear from his Word. If as a teenager I had rebelled against my father, I very well might have been confused about his will for me. For example, if I stayed out late each night, coming home only after Dad had gone to bed, and if I then got up after Dad left for work, I would never be in a position to hear him ask me to mow the grass. Or if loud music were blaring in my ear, then I could be in the same room with Dad and never hear his request.

Before I ask how to *know God's will*, I must first ask how well I *know him*. Am I putting myself in a position of personal contact with him? Am I getting rid of those things in my life that keep me from hearing his voice? If I'm walking close to God, then I need not fear that he is unable to communicate with me in unmistakable ways of his choosing, and I will never have to ask if he is leading me to serve in a particular way or place. Nothing can take away the joy of knowing that I'm where he wants me to be, doing what he wants me to do.

Answer from Mark Huddleston, who served with Pioneer Bible Translators in Zaire. He now serves as a professor at Nebraska Christian College.

A: Let God take you through the process he has for you.

The Bible teaches us that God is personal, that he created every one of us for a purpose, that he knows us, and that he wants the very best for us. Paul expresses it this way: "For we are God's workmanship, created in Christ Jesus to do good works, which God prepared in advance for us to do" (Ephesians 2:10).

The biblical writers also describe that although some people received concrete and definite direction from God, as did the apostle Paul when he received a vision (Acts 16:9), most people didn't. They had to ask God, trusting that he would guide them in his own way. For example, one writer says, "Trust in the Lord with all your heart and lean not on your own understanding; in all your ways acknowledge him, and he will make your paths straight" (Proverbs 3:5–6). This is usually a process. Turn from evil (Proverbs 3:7) and do right away what we know God wants.

The better we know him, the more we understand what pleases him. We will appreciate more and more his love for each individual and his longing for all peoples to know him, serve him, and enjoy his blessings. At the same time, we discover that he pushes us to grow in faith and gives us opportunities to obey him.

Answer from Jack Voelkel, missionary-in-residence with the Urbana Student Mission Convention. Previously Jack served thirty years with Latin America Mission in Peru and Colombia.

A: Ask yourself the hard questions.

Amy Carmichael was the founder of the Dohnavur Fellowship in India. When people wrote to her suggesting that they might like to come and work in India, she would ask three questions:

- Do you truly desire to live a crucified life?
- Does the thought of hardness draw you or repel you?
- Are you willing to do whatever helps most?

Amy established a wonderful home for children who otherwise would have been consigned to temple prostitution. Don't make up your mind that you are going to Africa or to China or to India to do a specific kind of work. In my experience, virtually all missionaries are asked to do many things not in their job description.

When Jim Elliot was considering missions, he didn't know where to go or what to do. But he did have two ideas. So he started corresponding with one missionary in India and another in Ecuador. In view of the information he received, he made a choice—Ecuador. But before deciding, he first did a lot of thinking and praying. It wasn't a wild guess but an act of faith in the God who promises to guide.

Jim used to say, "You can't steer a parked car." It makes sense to move in the direction you believe God is leading—trusting him as a faithful Shepherd to lead you in paths of righteousness.

Answer from Elisabeth Elliot, who worked with her husband Jim Elliot on translating the New Testament into the language of the Quichua Indians in Ecuador. Later, as a widow, she lived and worked among the Aucas.

A: Recognize the need. Realize that God has especially equipped you.

When I was trying to decide what to do with my life, I began to pray and meditate. But I didn't hear a voice, and I didn't see a verse jump out of my Bible. I simply received a growing realization that God was leading me to be a missionary. I think some make too much out of the concept of special direction to be a missionary.

Guidance is seeing a need and realizing that God has especially equipped you to meet that need. You discover a growing desire in your heart. And as you pursue that desire, you find a peace that surpasses understanding. His direction is confirmed as he opens the door and you walk through it.

When you follow God unreservedly, you give up control. Whatever it costs, boldly do whatever God wants you to do. The bottom line is not *where* you'll serve but *if* you'll go when he directs. God doesn't interview applicants for the position of missionary—he drafts them.

Answer from David Stevens, MD, who served eleven years at Tenwek Hospital in Kenya with World Medical Mission. David is CEO of the Christian Medical and Dental Associations.

A: Ask God to use you and watch him open doors.

Guidance is very personal. At a Christian university, I began to learn about missions and felt, like Paul, a strong desire to take the gospel where it had never been (Romans 15:20). Therefore, I asked God if I could become a missionary. While I didn't feel supernatural guidance, the interest certainly must have come from God.

After asking if I could be a missionary, I felt no negative response. So I simply began heading that way, and God opened doors. Over the next four years, I obtained the appropriate education and practical-ministry experience, and then I joined a mission.

Answer from David Smith, director of mobilization with WEC International. David has been a missionary for twenty-five years as a field worker in West Africa and at the WEC USA headquarters.

OPPOSITION AND OBSTACLES

Some circumstances and people encourage us into missions. But well-intentioned friends can also withhold encouragement—or even directly criticize—a desire for cross-cultural service. Let's sort through a series of specific obstacles that many have faced *and overcome* on their journey to becoming a missionary: friendly fire, fear, divorce, health, age, life mistakes, and lack of education. Look for answers that will help you personally and help you to encourage fellow prospective missionaries.

A: I did not anticipate friendly fire.

Spiritual attack will occur on those who begin to talk about engaging in kingdom expansion. Very often, especially early in our journey, the spiritual attack is what we might refer to as friendly fire. By that, I mean opposition comes from someone we would not normally expect, maybe a family or extended-family member, a friend, or someone in church or ministry leadership. We are surprised, maybe shocked, and quickly discouraged, feeling this just shouldn't be!

Often, the attack is an accusation, coming from people who know us and are believers. This is what can make it so discouraging. We think these people should be *for* us, but then we find them saying things *about* us that are unkind and usually untrue. Friendly fire. What should we do?

First, we do what Scripture instructs us to do: stand firm. This means we do not quit and run. Nor do we try to attack. We stand firm:

- **Firm in the conviction** that we are being obedient to God's direction in our life;
- **Firm in our faith** that God knows exactly what is happening and knows how to protect us;
- **Firm in our commitment** to follow Jesus, regardless of the cost;
- **Firm in our understanding** that the enemy will flee as we resist him (James 4:7).

This topic is one of the themes discussed in The Journey Deepens weekend retreats for prospective missionaries.

Answer from Don Parrott, who has served in missions for twenty-five years with OC International in Argentina and Guatemala and with Paraclete and Finishers Project in the United States.

A: I did not know if I would be an effective missionary.

Though my heart was full of desire to go, my mind was full of doubts about my ability to make a real difference in the lives of Albanian people.

Over the years, my doubts have remained. I look at what I've done, and on one hand, I'm satisfied with the ministries I've started and helped others plug into. On the other hand, I realize that whatever good I've done—whether it be the number of ministries started or souls won to Christ—must be viewed in the light of my degree of surrender to Christ. My doubts have served as a thorn so that my sense of accomplishment may not rest on my good works but on Christ and his righteousness.

I think our longevity in missions depends on our sense of dependency on God's grace. Our doubts, whether they be in feeling inadequate or in another area, are necessary for us to remain qualified for the tasks before us.

Answer from Nathan in Albania, who has served with Christar for fifteen years.

Q: How can I prepare for missions when others try to discourage me?

A: Listen; be patient; read the Psalms.

It's not surprising that the enemy might want to dissuade us, and sometimes he even uses those around us. The way to defeat him is not to rail against individuals but to call on the name of the Lord, ask for his protection, claim his armor (Ephesians 6), and trust him to make all things work together for good (Romans 8:28).

The Scripture says, "Wounds from a friend can be trusted" (Proverbs 27:6). Listen carefully to the criticisms of your detractors, even if they come across as harsh. Their criticisms may contain some truth. Ask older, wise friends to help you learn from what you're hearing others say. People often don't say things to our faces because they lack the courage; therefore, they talk behind our backs. However, we still need to learn from their words. None of us is perfect, and the Lord uses many different experiences to shape us.

Above all, ask the Lord for patience. Perhaps the Lord is preparing you for missionary service through this experience. You will suffer far worse opportunities for discouragement once you get involved in cross-cultural missionary activity! Staying humble, not talking back, learning from criticism, and placing this situation before the Lord are powerful means of spiritual growth.

Spend time reading the Psalms. Note how the psalmist experienced attack after attack, even from his closest friends.

Answer from Jack Voelkel.

Editor's Note: For discussions on opposition to missionary service from family—a spouse, parents, teenagers, and adult children—see chapter 6, "Singles, Couples, and Kids."

A: Discouragement is a part of life.

We live in a fallen world, and things such as discouragement happen. This is true for all of us. The key is to stay close to Jesus Christ. Spend quality and quantity time reading his Word, praying, and waiting on him—communicating with our commander in chief.

Part of the problem is often low self-esteem, also a result of our fallen world. Deal with childhood and other issues. We all have some. See a Christian counselor if necessary, and learn to trust Jesus in everything and for everything no matter how dark the path may seem.

Pray in the name of Jesus against Satan and his hosts, commanding them to leave you. Not all discouragement is from our enemy. But it's good to pray against this possibility, and it's good to put him in his place.

Call upon the Lord and spend time praising him. Ask for strength and peace and joy that only he brings. And may the God of peace be with you.

Answer from Denis Shuker, a recruiter and sender with OMS International.

Editor's Note: Perhaps we should ignore the traditional expectation that missionaries have to be superspiritual, with no questions or problems when it comes to handling relationships, caring for family members, or knowing how to live in another culture.

Sometimes missionary life, however, gets so relationally and practically challenging that only a superb sense of humor will pull us through. Author Sue Eenigenburg lists in her missionary blockbuster *Screams in the Desert* (see "Resources for Further Study") chapters entitled "Diarrhea and Team Life," "Terrorists and Chocolate Cake," "Suicide and Laundry," and "Listen, God,

I'm Speaking."

Sue tells of her early reactions to the challenge of missionary life:

> One night, as my husband and I snuggled in bed (when the air conditioner was actually on), we were discouraged about living out of trunks, getting cheated by almost everyone, getting stared at by everyone else, and fighting the dirt, the bugs and the traffic. I asked him if we could go home. He said that we could as long as I was the one who would repack everything and then I, only I, would have to carry the trunks.[1]

Consequently, for the following twelve years of missionary life, Sue stayed.

Q: Can I become a missionary if I fear going overseas?

A: Look to Jesus and read my story.

As a young adult, I talked with different team leaders to see which country I would go to. I met Norm, who led the team going to Sudan. That trip seemed like more an adventure than all the others. But in my last interview with Norm, he looked me in the eye and asked, "Are you ready to die in Sudan?" I remember thinking, *Look buddy, I'm here for one year, got it? I am engaged to a beautiful girl back home. I've got a life and a future waiting for me. No one has asked me to die for anything before!*

I went away and thought and even prayed about this. I kept thinking that no one had ever asked me that before—but then it hit me hard. Someone *had* asked me. It was Jesus.

I went to Sudan. It was the most difficult, purging time of my life. I came back broken. I was a different man for Rachael when I returned. In my heart was placed a flame—a burning desire for Muslim people that cannot be quenched. That was twenty-two years ago. Now the flame burns hotter and deeper. Rachael and I never accomplished my original career plan to run a beautiful Christian camp in the Rockies. Instead, God has taken us to North Africa, the Middle East, and the Arabian Peninsula. Here we will stay by his grace until he releases us or takes us home.[2]

Answer from Keith and Rachael, who serve in the Arab world with Operation Mobilization.

Q. Can I become a missionary even though I am divorced?

A: Yes, even if you have remarried.

A decade or two ago, the answer would have been a definite no. But that has changed, and many mission agencies will consider each case individually. Among the missionaries in the country where I work, there is a divorced single man and a divorced and remarried woman. Start inquiring, and don't be discouraged if you get some negative answers. Keep at it, because there are agencies that want you.

Answer from Jennifer, serving in West Africa with United World Mission.

Q: Can I become a missionary even if I have some health problems?

A: Probably. Even disabled persons are missionaries.

Years ago, mission service was limited to healthy young people—anyone over the age of thirty need not apply. Today, the mission world values the maturity that accompanies age and infirmity, so retirees, second-career professionals, and even disabled persons are welcomed.

I know disabled missionaries working in third-world countries. For example, a wheelchair-bound young woman works in a small Senegalese town, and a man paralyzed from the waist down serves in South America. I also know of some people whose children have life-threatening diseases, and they still served effectively for many years. You might expect people with health problems to serve only in large cities, but that is not always the case. Look for an organization that can effectively place you and will work with your limitation—and your strengths.

Answer from Jennifer, serving in West Africa with United World Mission.

Q: Can I become a missionary if I am over forty years old?

A: It's never too late.

I was a mechanical engineer, and my wife was an elementary school teacher. At the time, we had mountainous debt and no theological training. Then over seven years, we eliminated our debt, studied the Bible for a year, found a mission agency, raised full support, and then left for the desert of northwest Kenya. We've never been sorry, and we've never thought we were too old.

God led us to a mission agency that believes second-career missionaries bring valuable maturity and life experience to missions, contributions not available from younger graduates. In recent years, more agencies have begun to appreciate these same values and have become part of Finishers Project. Visit finishers.org for resources and a job-matching service. Enter information about your experience to find organizations with opportunities that fit your training, skills, and interests.

Answer from Jeff, who has served in Africa for nine years with United World Mission.

Q. ■ **Can I become a missionary**
■ **even though I've made a ton of**
mistakes in life?

A: ■ Yes!

Be encouraged! It's only by the grace of God that any of us are in one piece. One of the messages of a missionary is "If God can heal me, he can heal you as well." Your difficulties can make you more real and understanding and can help you relate to those who are suffering.

Beware: going to a different country must not be a means of hiding from your problems at home. If left unresolved, problems will haunt you in missions. Being immersed in a new culture and a new language is stressful enough, and just as a dike holds back a flood, powerful stresses highlight breaking points that seemed insignificant before the waters started rising. If your relationship with your parents is not healthy, for example, you could easily find yourself in trouble overseas.

God has always chosen to use broken people to do his work. Gaining humility is a crucial step to being used by God. As long as you are submissive to the Holy Spirit, there is nothing to stop you. I would suggest you find a mentor who can help you deal with some of these issues and who can force you to be honest.

Answer from Jack Voelkel.

Q: Can I become a missionary if I have limited education?

A: Yes. I'm a missionary even though I am dyslexic.

I am dyslexic, and I can't spell to save a life (praise God for computers with spell check). I speak Portuguese badly and can't write it. My main ministry is church planting and Bible school. I love the local people, and I know they love me in return. Often a person who "has it all" misses being one with the people.

Our African director has the same problem I do and is being used greatly by the Lord in Kenya. If God is leading you to become a missionary, do not be afraid to go. He will guide and lead. If he can use a donkey, he can use me.

Answer from Paul, who has served as a missionary in Mozambique for twelve years.

A: Yes. Your relationship with the Lord means more than ability.

Some believe that God selects those who are qualified. I think, however, that he qualifies those he selects. No matter what disabilities we have—and all of us have them—God can use us. Education seems much more important to first-world people. We in Latin America think what is most important is God's direction and your relationship with him—no matter your ability or education.

Answer from Moisés in Mexico.

THE WAYS AND MEANS OF SERVICE

Perhaps you're wondering if it would be selfish or just more realistic to stay in your home country and find some way to get involved in missions without having to move internationally. Be encouraged. God has many ways for us to participate in his mission story. Each role is vital to the Lord of the harvest, whether that role is serving in a land foreign to your own or serving in your hometown. People *everywhere* need to know life in Jesus.

The apostle Paul reminds us in 1 Corinthians 12 that all parts together make a whole body—inner parts, outer parts, prominent parts, lesser parts. All are needed. It's the same with missions. Let's explore various ways and means of mission service.

Q: I don't sense God leading me to become a missionary. Is it selfish for me to send financial and prayer support and not go myself?

A: Not at all. Be a sender.

We have all been called to the body of Christ and to function within that body. Some will be witnesses in Jerusalem (your hometown); some will be witnesses in Judea (linking arms in a greater area ministry). Some will be witnesses in Samaria (among the "unlovables" of the world), and some, as they are going throughout the world, will be witnesses to the uttermost parts.

For those who go to the uttermost parts, there is a need for a support team—a care group. For every military personnel who goes to the front line of battle, a minimum of nine people back him up on the line of communication. Those who serve as senders are equally important. Their responsibilities are quite different from those who go, but they are equally vital. No, it is not selfish to be a part of the rest of the team. Imagine a baseball coach telling the right fielder, "Hey, you didn't touch the ball the whole game. We don't need you anymore!" Of course not. Likewise, though the ones who go might be like a pitcher or a catcher who touches the ball every inning, the other members of the team are equally responsible to fulfill their particular role.

On the other hand, we see an interesting progression in Matthew 9–10. Jesus has called on his followers to "ask the Lord of the harvest to send out workers into his harvest field" (9:38). A few verses later he seems to tell his followers, "OK, guys. You're it. Get going!" It may be that as you have been faithful in providing financial and prayer support for your missionary friend, God will direct you to the front line yourself.

Answer from Neal Pirolo, missionary trainer and author of Serving As Senders.

Q: Can I serve international missions and still live full-time in my home country?

A: Yes.

God has brought the internationals of the world to the doorsteps of the developed world. To serve an international student in your area, contact a Christian ministry at a university near you.

Another way to serve at home is to learn about missionaries from your church who serve internationally. Get to know them, what they do, and how you can support them financially, spiritually, and practically. More information can be found in Neal Pirolo's book *Serving As Senders* (see "Resources for Further Study").

There are always options to go on a short-term mission trip overseas during your vacation. And most important, pray for the world. Find a group that meets to pray for a people group or an area of the world.

Answer from Karin, who serves in Germany with Youth With A Mission.

A: Work at an international office in your home country.

Many mission agencies have offices in your home country. Those of us working in the home office serve as a lifeline of support for missionaries overseas. You can serve in personnel, recruiting, fund-raising, finance, payroll, computers/IT, publicity, marketing, or a dozen other areas. In many agencies, you would need to raise your own support, just as someone serving in another country does (but hey, that's fair to those overseas). An army has to have its supply lines, and so does God's army of missionaries. Check with the home office of the agencies you might want to serve with to see what positions they need to fill.

Answer from Rob, who served ten years with Operation Mobilization from the home office.

Q: Can I use my professional or technical skills as a missionary?

A: Sometimes.

The church needs more Christians who will serve in the professions, business, and the trades. Since the work environment provides intimate contact with a small cadre of co-workers, you can live out your faith in real life through your profession.

First, learn about the area where you want to go: the needs and strengths of the country and the region, work permits available to foreigners, and the work environment of your profession. Is your experience useful there? How is your profession or skill performed there? What kinds of office politics and bureaucratic red tape drive projects?

I recommend you contact Global Opportunities (globalopps.org) to learn more. They are a terrific outfit with experience in counseling and placing people in many parts of the world.

Answer from Jack Voelkel.

Editor's Note: For questions and answers about using your university major or professional skill in missions, visit AskAMissionary. com > Professional Skills. Also, read Patrick Lai's book *Tentmaking: Business as Missions* (see "Resources for Further Study").

WHERE IN THE WORLD?

While there are important ways to be involved with missions from home, many discover that going in person to another culture is both fulfilling and strategic. But with so many service opportunities around the world, how do you pick just one? Or do you wait for God to give you a final destination before you begin to prepare?

All missionaries have wrestled with these questions; that's common ground they share with you. What's not common, however, is how, when, and where God leads each one. No one-size-fits-all here, no set-in-stone method by which God leads. But be assured, he does lead!

Here are some different experiences and approaches by which missionaries have found how, when, and where in the world God wanted them to serve.

Q: Should I wait for guidance to a specific country?

A: Let God direct you where and how he pleases.

Don't let this worry you. We are all different. Missionary biographies are replete with those who had a lifetime direction to a particular people, for example, Hudson Taylor's call to the Chinese. Others, such as C. T. Studd, moved around. Did Paul have direction to a particular culture or geographical location? He went as the Spirit led him.

My own direction came as a child. I knew God wanted me to be a missionary. I thought it was going to be in Korea, but God shut that door. Through a chain of circumstances, he led me first to Canada, then to Latin America in general and university students in particular. Thirty years in Colombia have made these people very dear to us, but we lived in four countries and served in many others. He will lay the burdens on our hearts when and how he pleases, as we are open to him.

God's basic guidance is to know and serve him—the place is secondary. We served the Lord for many years among students in Colombia, South America. I once asked Eugenio, who worked for several years among indigenous peoples, how he happened into cross-cultural ministry. He replied, "Well, you got us involved in serving the people next to us, then you took us to universities where there was no witness, and you never told us when to stop."

As we seek God's will, it's helpful to analyze who we are—our abilities, our interests, our opportunities, what gives us the greatest joy, and the tug of our hearts—as well as to ask the counsel of wise friends we respect. As we bring these resources before the Lord in prayer and get involved in serving him where we are, we can expect him to show us with increasing clarity the next steps.

Answer from Jack Voelkel.

A: No. Ask God to first match you to a mission agency.

Mission statesman Ralph Winter used a sports analogy: what team you're playing on is more important than the stadium in which you are playing. Let the Lord decide where he wants to place you in his world. Perhaps you have a clear, specific geographic interest, and that will focus your selection of an agency. But for most, God has given gifts and a desire to respond. For example, about half of those who join WEC International don't begin with a geographical interest, but they know they're being led into missions and to that agency.

Some agencies have global opportunities, so you can find a placement anywhere in the world. Other groups have a geographical focus, such as Greater Europe Mission. The agency name may or may not indicate that focus. For example, Christian Associates International also works mainly in Europe.

Answer from John McVay, mission mobilizer with In His Image International Medical Missions and The Journey Deepens retreats for prospective missionaries.

A: No. Expect a God-given curiosity to be your first step to the nations.

Christians in the West have for generations talked about missions mostly in terms of being called to political countries. The Bible, however, tells us to make disciples among all nations, using the

Greek term *ethne*—or "ethnic groups." For example, in the political country of Sudan, there are more than five hundred distinct ethnic groups. So how does God lead you to a particular group?

Missiologist Herbert Kane interviewed hundreds of missionaries about their sense of a missionary call to a place or a people. He found that what they referred to in hindsight as a call was most often a sequence of curiosity, interest, understanding, assurance, conviction, commitment, and finally the action of moving out to live among a particular people.

So instead of waiting for some kind of traditional "call" to some specific place or people, it makes all kinds of sense to follow your God-given curiosity and interests—and "look among the nations" (Habakkuk 1:5 ESV).

Answer from Bill Stearns, author of 2020 Vision and missionary trainer with Finishers Project.

Q. How do I discover which country or people group God is leading me to serve?

A: Reflect on how you could serve in missions.

Begin with the promise of Psalm 32:8: "I will instruct you and teach you in the way you should go; I will counsel you and watch over you."

Look to God as your Father and your Master. It is a father's responsibility to give guidance to a child, and a master's responsibility to give guidance to a servant or slave. Your responsibility is to seek God's will with a determination to obey.

However, I do have a suggestion. Ask yourself, *When I simply daydream, what do I see myself doing as a missionary?* Do you see yourself caring for children? Then find what missions have special ministries to children. Do you see yourself in open evangelism and discipleship? Then look to a country open to the gospel, which includes many countries in Latin America, Europe, Africa, and Asia. Do you see yourself more involved in discreet one-to-one ministry? Then you're probably looking at some ministry in a more difficult country. Do you see yourself more with Africans, Asians, Europeans, or Middle Eastern peoples? Do you have a particular burden for one religious group?

As you work to answer several of these questions, some ideas should come to mind. You may also want to ask other people to help you evaluate your spiritual gifts to see in what setting these may seem appropriate.

Finally, get the book *Operation World* (see "Resources for Further Study") and begin reading about the countries of the world. Hundreds of people have been directed toward specific nations, people groups, and ministries through this book.

Answer from David Smith, director of mobilization with WEC International. David has been a missionary for twenty-five years as a field worker in West Africa and at the WEC USA headquarters.

 Consider countries with the greatest need.

Jesus is doing amazing things in an amazingly desperate world. I encourage you to look overseas, where, any way you put it, the need is much greater than in the West. Consider these indications of need (or lack of):

- **Nutrition.** A homeless person in Los Angeles gets more calories of quality food per day than the average person in Calcutta.

- *Justice*. Fifteen million children are sold into sexual slavery each year, primarily in Asia.
- *Access to the gospel*. There are more Bibles, Christian books, and Christian radio stations in North America than we know what to do with. In any city in the United States, you are never more than a mile from a church.

Answer from Jack Voelkel.

Q: Should I go on a short-term mission trip just to try it out?

A: Yes, but go for several months.

I know that some people say that a short-term trip is not necessary to confirm God's direction for you into missions. I would say, however, it can be helpful to go for several months—even six months to a year if possible.

Although I had guidance to go into missions since my midteens, short-term trips changed my ideas concerning what tasks or role I should be doing in missions. I actually changed my career direction completely: I have medical training but am now doing surveys for future Bible translations.

Answer from Mike, who served ten years in West Africa and North Africa on a Bible translation team with WEC International.

A: Yes. Strategically select your short-term mission.

It may be a good idea to go on a short-term mission trip. First, determine what information you need regarding the long-term direction you sense from the Holy Spirit. For example, how could your spiritual gifts and vocational skills be used in a particular field, and what language skills are necessary?

Then talk with several agencies to seek a fit between your gifts, skills, and direction and the agencies' short-term opportunities. Determine whether the short-term trip will stimulate career missionary work or if it's just a one-time project. Make sure there is a debriefing opportunity with someone in the agency to help you decide your next step in missions.

Answer from Jim Hogrefe, regional director for OMS International. Previously he served in Russia for two years.

A: Perhaps go for the long-term track from the start.

If you are reasonably sure God wants you in long-term missions, go for the long-term track right from the start. It will save you in the end and get you on course right away.

If you're not sure but are open to being shown with a heart to follow fully, then a short-term experience in an area of the world in which you have an interest, or to a ministry for which you have a heart, is a good approach.

Answer from Merle, who served for twenty-one years in Ethiopia and Sudan with Serving in Mission (SIM).

THE TIME IS RIGHT

Alongside the question of "Where?" come the questions "How long do I stay?" and "When do I go?" This is when the stories get really exciting—reading of God's miraculous, amazing timing for each missionary. After all, he is the creator and keeper of time. Get ready to hear the wise instruction of those who know firsthand God's perfect and faithful guidance. Though the timing for each was different, it was, well . . . right on time!

Q: How long should I plan to go— one year, two years, or longer?

A: Start with two years.

Here are some reasons to start with at least a two-year commitment:

- **Incarnation**. Jesus modeled for us how to do ministry and mission. Two years is long enough to live among a people, develop relationships, and allow them to see and know Christ.
- **Life transformation**. In ways that short-term missions cannot, two years is long enough to develop habits, faith postures, and global paradigms that affect how we see the world and how we live the rest of our lives.
- **Life direction**. We can seize longer seasons in life, such as the time between jobs or before launching a career, to

go and help. These extended, opportune times can propel our understanding and involvement in our role in God's global purpose.

Answer from Ryan, who is serving in Central Asia with Pioneers.

Q: How can I know God's timing?

A: Trust and wait.

We serve a God who knows each heart. So as you speak with other missionaries, you may be surprised to learn that his guidance is different for each life. My husband and I were both children when we caught a vision for China. We met about fifteen years later, began a friendship, and later married. But it took another ten years before we arrived in China. Why did it take so long? I have no idea, but when we went, it was so right!

Pray each day about your burden for missions. God will speak to you through his Word, through the Holy Spirit in your times of prayer, and through other Christians in your life.

Answer from Karin, who served as an English teacher in China for five years.

A: Wait on God to confirm his direction in multiple ways.

We believe that big moves require big confirmations, and God is faithful to provide them. We must have a heart assurance of God's direction to endure the inherent difficulties and sacrifices that come with missions. For those who are married, this must be true for both husband and wife.

For some, this process will be more mystical in nature than for others. Though a mystical sense of God's leading in our hearts is desirable, doing something as drastic as becoming a long-term missionary on only a whim or a feeling often produces disastrous results over time.

Take incremental steps in your inquiries of your church, friends, and mission agencies, trusting God to open or shut doors as he sees fit. Look for specific and obvious answers to prayer concerning your move. Often, circumstances will line up in an unusual and revealing way, indicating God's favor toward a specific move.

In our case, we recorded all of the small, circumstantial "miracles" God did to get us to Spain; for example, the miraculous way our house sold. By the time we arrived in Spain, there were twenty such confirmations, which we kept on file just in case we ever began to doubt God's hand in this assignment. This assurance was a source of strength, comfort, and peace. God is good to us, and being a missionary is a great honor well worth any sacrifice for him and worth the time it may take to hear his voice.

Answer from David Nelson, who served for thirteen years in Spain, planting churches with Elim Fellowship.

A: 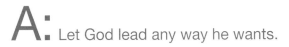 Let God lead any way he wants.

Three different times my wife and I launched into full-time mission work.

During one short-term trip, we visited a number of ministries in South America. On one of those visits, I simply realized, *We can do this!* My wife and I returned home, and after some prayer and counsel with godly friends we applied to the agency. And they sent us.

Years later, while out of steady work, we were seeking the Lord for his direction in further ministry. I (foolishly, in some people's eyes) passed by a number of opportunities that seemed so right. At the time, I couldn't give a definitive reason for my delaying. However, when later invited into the office of a mission agency, the answer became clear: they had an emergency need. Ten weeks later, my wife and I and our four children were overseas again, filling a critical need.

During yet another season of life, I struggled when I learned that the man for whom I was working no longer wanted me. Though I survived physically, I was an emotional wreck. I needed more than scriptural assurance of God's will for my life. I needed a fleece! Yes, like Gideon, my emotions needed a sign. I said, "Lord, if you really mean for me to be in ministry, without me doing anything to make it happen, I need to see three things: The name for the ministry, the thrust of the ministry, and the logo." Twenty-eight days later, in my regular morning reading of the Word, the Lord did just that!

Answer from Neal Pirolo.

A: Draw closer to God and trust him.

God honors obedience. He is in your life, ready to lead you according to his program of guidance. Ask yourself if your motivation in life is to glorify God. Often the struggles we have with situations do not grow out of love for God but out of selfishness and pride.

We are easily influenced subjectively by all kinds of motives. That's why it is so helpful when facing significant decisions to take time to meditate on Scripture, consult with wise Christian friends, and continue to trust God.

Often we put our focus on the immediate issue rather than on our relationship to the Lord. Finding God's guidance is more a matter of drawing close to him than just finding the "magic answer" to individual questions.

Sometimes the Lord pushes us in one direction so that we'll have a different perspective than what we otherwise could have had. Regardless, he does not abandon us, even when we feel con-fused. In times of confusion, our tendency is to panic. A more help-ful response is to sit down, bring the whole issue before the Lord, review the past, and then ask how we should proceed, recognizing that his continued goal is to foster with us a closer relationship of obedience, trust, and dependence on him.

God is never in a hurry, but he is sometimes silent (which can be irritating), and we occasionally experience confusion. But through it all, he is training us, leading us, and teaching us lessons of faith.

Answer from Jack Voelkel.

MY THOUGHTS SO FAR

With all the wise counsel you've just picked up in this chapter, now's a good time to think through your own answers to the questions just discussed. So ask the Holy Spirit to guide you, through God's Word and through prayer. Answer each question in light of what you *currently* understand from God.

If you don't receive complete answers to every question about God's guidance, don't panic. He leads us into life's next steps when we're ready and when we're spiritually clean and open to him. His guidance might be one step at a time. Or he might reveal a fresh vision of our pathway in the years ahead.

As you explore your role in God's mission story, discuss your responses to the questions below with a leader or friend in your local church.

How do I believe God typically guides believers into new areas of service?

_____

_____

_____

Is God leading me to become a missionary? What confirmations have I received?

_____

_____

_____

Do I sense God leading me to work in international missions in my home country? In what ways could I serve here?

_____

_____

_____

_____

Do I sense God leading me to work in a specific country or people group? If so, which country or people group? What confirmations have I received?

_____

_____

_____

_____

What type of strategic focus does my church have with a particular city, nation, or unreached people group?

_____

_____

_____

What are my obstacles to becoming a missionary? How will I respond to the obstacles and to people who try to discourage me?

_____

_____

_____

Should I go on a short-term mission trip just to try it out?

_____

_____

How long should I plan to go—one year, two years, or longer?

_____

_____

What do I sense from God is the right timing for me to go into missions?

_____

_____

_____

My specific prayer to God about my involvement in his mission is:

_____

_____

_____

I will use the following two resources to learn more about missions and God's guidance (find ideas in "Resources for Further Study" at the end of this book):

1. _____

_____

2. _____

_____

AGENCIES
Researching the Options

3

A DOWNPOUR OF THE NORTH AFRICAN SUN SHONE
on the old dual-cab compact pickup. I swiped at the yellow paint—
which was, instead, yellow dirt from the latest sandstorm. Here
in Mauritania, peanut butter comes in huge cans with red plastic
lids that make great taillights when duct-taped to the frame. There
aren't many auto-parts stores in this corner of the world.

I asked Brent about a long gouge across the passenger-side
door.

He squinted at the damaged door. "I think it came during a
medical-evacuation trip to a village, driving on a motorbike path.
Or . . . maybe it was a birthing trip, when, as in an ambulance,
our nurse has the pregnant woman stretch out in the back of the
pickup on the way to the clinic. Nine times out of ten, the nurse
bangs on the cab window for the driver to stop. This old pickup
has been the delivery room for, oh, a dozen newborns so far."

"And the fender?"

"A disagreement over right of way—with a cow."

From my list, I counted the number of missionaries and kids
traveling tomorrow—in this hopefully reliable pickup—to our
agency field conference, a sort of missionary family reunion.

Brent, Debbie, plus toddler.

Paul, Carol, and toddler.

Jim, Dena, and teen-aged son Kris.

Short-term volunteer Todd.

Me.

"So, Brent, we've got ten people going to the field conference tomorrow. How long is the drive?"

Brent tilted his head. "Twelve hours probably, so we'll leave before sunup. But we'll drop you and the women and children off at the closest airstrip. It's too far and too risky for the whole group to travel across the desert, so you all will fly most of the way to the conference."

The next morning, the ten of us stood around the pickup, excited and guessing at who could sit where. With the luggage and food, no matter how we squeezed, only seven could fit inside. The others would have to ride in the back "birthing room."

Shivering in the pre-dawn desert darkness, we prayed around the old truck; then we took our positions. Jim drove, with Brent riding next to him. The three women and two toddlers sat in the backseat, juggling hot cinnamon rolls and coffee cups on their laps. Paul, Kris, Todd, and I stood in the back, desperately holding on to the bars of the overhead luggage rack as we bounced along the dirt track toward the nearest town.

As we neared that town around dawn, a police officer ahead of us marched into the road and flagged down our pickup. Paul raised his eyebrows and said to me. "I've never seen the police here." Stepping to Jim's window, the officer said, *"Vos documents, s'il vous plaît."* Then he glared through the window, counted those of us in the truck bed, widened his eyes, and spat out, *"Documents, Monsieur!"*

Jim, obviously nervous, simply said, *"Je ne vous comprends pas."* I don't understand.

Quick-thinking Debbie called out from the backseat, *"Monsieur!"* and handed the officer a huge cinnamon roll.

The officer then stepped back, smiled, and took the roll. *"Allez, Allez."* And he waved us on.

We stopped at the airstrip just outside of town, and the women, children, and I climbed aboard a roaring prop plane. Feeling thankful for the ease of flying the rest of the way—and a little guilty—we waved to the men and shouted above the roar that we'd meet up at the conference.

Darkness drops fast across the African sky. From the conference grounds, we strained to keep sight of the horizon, watching for the men to arrive from their cross-desert drive. I stood, freshly showered, with the wives, children, and other missionaries who had already arrived from other parts of Mauritania. I had to ask, "Isn't this too risky and a lot of effort just to get missionaries from the agency together? I mean, I'm sure it'll be a good time, but . . ."

Incredulous that I would even ask the question, Debbie sputtered, "All this effort? And risk?" But then she heard a muffler backfire and saw the headlights of the yellow-encrusted, dual-cab compact pickup. And she declared, "We need each other."

Everyone clapped in agreement, joyful to get to spend the week playing and praying together.

In a split second, my mind flipped through all the conventional stories of lonely, isolated missionaries living on the edge of survival. I decided in that moment that I too would cross the widest desert for respite and renewal with my missionary family. Why? Because we need each other.

BENEFITS OF AN AGENCY

By now, you may be ready to explore in depth how to become a missionary. A critical next step is determining if God wants you to serve independently or with a mission agency. In this chapter, experienced missionaries explain the benefits of both and give critical questions for you to ask a potential mission agency.

Remember the inspiring stories of missionary pioneers quavering in loneliness and isolation? Today, serving the God of billions means you don't have to be a lone ranger in mission ministry. Teamwork is increasingly the norm for today's missionary.

First, let's explore the option of mission work facilitated through the skills, interest, and care of missionary-sending agencies.

Q: Why do many missionaries join agencies?

A: Because agencies help missionaries be more effective.

Agencies differ, but most of them offer these services:

- *Placement*. They tell you about openings in the countries where they work.
- *Financial support*. Agencies usually require you to raise

your own financial support. However, they guide you in this process, giving you materials to give to potential supporters and helping you describe what you'll be doing. Once you're accepted by the agency, they provide your supporters with tax-deductible receipts.

- **Orientation**. Crossing cultures is a demanding experience, both intellectually and emotionally. Good mission agencies can be of great help, since they know the culture where you'll be going and how best to prepare you. They will recommend a language-training option and help you find your way around the country.

- **Supervision**. We all need supervision to guide us in our work, help us learn from our mistakes, and encourage our development.

- **Member care**. Early mission pioneers were pretty much on their own. Now, more mission agencies look out for their people: their spiritual needs, their intellectual growth, their plans for furlough, the education of their children, and their preparation for retirement.

Answer from Jack Voelkel, missionary-in-residence with the Urbana Student Mission Convention. Previously Jack served thirty years with Latin America Mission in Peru and Colombia.

A: For encouragement by a team on the field.

I've done it both ways. But I feel it's important to be part of a mission organization. You face so many new situations when you're serving in another culture, and being on a team (when it's functioning properly) provides the support and counsel needed in those situations. I've also found the fellowship of other missionaries to be invaluable, even when there were tensions to be worked out. It's also beneficial to be in close communication with one's sending church. Your home church needs to know how important it is for them to stay involved and to communicate with you.

Answer from Barbara in Tulsa, who served for five years as a missionary in Israel, Russia, and India.

A: Because our church has learned that missionaries need an agency.

We decided to send our missionaries directly to other countries without the help of an agency. Looking back, we were quite naive. We thought that sending people for longer terms would not involve any challenges different from short terms. We were wrong.

We first sent two women to Panama. Immediately we encountered numerous complicated background checks and bureaucratic paperwork to acquire their visas. Then we needed to consider where to secure medical insurance and a pension plan.

We also sent my grown son to minister in Ecuador. He coordinated our incoming short-term teams. One day while he was traveling on a bus, bandits hijacked the bus and forced everyone out for a couple of hours. While we were thankful that no one was hurt, we realized that we could encounter an even more difficult political upheaval. We knew that if our missionaries were ever taken hostage, we lacked the expertise to deal with foreign governments or terrorists.

We decided that we indeed needed mission agencies through which to send our people. Agencies offer the church wise placement of workers, expertise on the field, and contacts in the host country. So we earnestly began looking for agencies willing to partner with us. We found one in particular that is proving to be an excellent fit. It has also developed ways for missionaries to receive quality training in shorter stints, closer to home.

I would encourage the church that is considering sending longer-term missionaries without an agency's help to exercise extreme caution. Such a church is shouldering a tremendous responsibility for its missionaries' safety, health, and supervision in ministry. It's a big task for which few churches are prepared. We are a church of eight thousand. We are well staffed and financed for missions, yet we found that we weren't equipped for the job of mission agency.[1]

Answer from Porter Speakman, missions pastor at Central Church of God in Charlotte, North Carolina.

A: For prayer support.

To not have a mission agency is asking for disaster. An agency is responsible not only to pray and organize prayer support but also to make sure that prayer is directed to specific needs. The agency can provide a large part of the prayer covering that a missionary must have in order to do kingdom work. To select a mission agency takes time and prayer. It must be a good fit for both the agency and for you. Sometimes things work for a while, but then you have to change agencies. Every agency will have some things that may not perfectly suit your situation, but then no pair of shoes ever fits exactly. Shoes do not fit perfectly because of the imperfect feet in them.

Answer from Jim, who served as an English teacher in China for five years.

A: For preparation and teamwork.

Some independent missionaries have very good ministries. However, some independents seem to be content to reinvent the wheel and make mistakes that others could have warned them about. Here are some benefits of going with a mission agency:

- *Pre-field preparation*. Most agencies require their missionaries to train from a few intense weeks to several months, studying different issues such as cross-cultural adjustment, anthropology, mission strategy, and church planting.

- **Strategic planning**. A mission agency can give you a clear understanding of its work with the particular people group or country of your interest and connect you with workers already there. This helps avoid silly mistakes in planning. For example, an independent missionary couple came to the country where I work without trying to learn French, which is the national language. They thought they would work through translators (which, by the way, works well in some countries). However, missionaries here lose credibility with the people if they refuse to learn French.

- **Accountability**. Many people have trouble planning their time, using it wisely, and knowing how to evaluate goals. With an agency, several missionaries working in the same area can keep each other accountable and on track. Also, falling into temptation is easier in isolated situations, where missionaries are lone rangers and think they won't be caught.

- **Encouragement**. Within an agency, missionaries share the same ethos of mission, and they encourage and pray with each other in the hard times. Yes, we can always e-mail friends back home, but it's really nice to have a flesh-and-blood person available to hear our concerns.

- **Freedom for ministry**. Usually, an agency has several staff members to take care of matters that would consume our time if we had to do it ourselves. This help might include buying airplane tickets, transferring money, obtaining certain supplies, and keeping track of our finances. In developing countries, business is often conducted in the capital city. Weeks of time can be lost having to make frequent trips to the capital to take care of business matters. An agency's personnel can free us for ministry.

- **Teamwork**. The New Testament concept of evangelism and church planting usually involved teamwork. Today, a team concept can offer many benefits. (1) Working in fellowship, a team has the potential to model Christian community for a lost world, especially a team of inter-nationals working together. (2) A team can give different perspectives on the work. (3) The Bible teaches that in joining together, our potential increases exponentially. (4) Other people working with us from our sending agency can offset our weaknesses. (5) Other people can help continue a ministry we started if we must return to our home country.
- **Response in crisis**. An agency usually has a network of workers within a country that is up-to-date on our lives and work. If a personal crisis occurs or an outside threat is imminent, the mission can provide prompt response with personnel on the spot.

Answer from Mike, who served ten years in West Africa and North Africa on a Bible translation team with WEC International.

A: Because it's biblical—and practical too.

In Acts 13, we find the formation of the first mission team and first agency. The team, Paul and Barnabas, was not micromanaged from Antioch. They were capable Christian workers who had proved their ministry and were sent to do God's bidding. But just as Paul and Barnabas were careful to keep ties with Antioch on their return, so is it incumbent on mission agencies to maintain healthy ties with their denomination or local church. We are all members of the larger body of Christ. Interrelatedness is essential to effectiveness.

Agencies can and should provide experience and expertise in reaching their target people groups. Reputable agencies will be members of the Mission Exchange, CrossGlobal Link, or a similar association. They will be financially accountable, with books audited by an independent organization. Agencies will provide in-depth training in culture, language, spiritual discipleship, and the evangelistic methods proven effective in their particular venues. Of course, if an agency is new, then its leadership ought to have a proven record in ministry.

Answer from Jack Chapin in Indianapolis, a church consultant with Arab World Ministries.

BENEFITS OF INDEPENDENT SERVICE

After reading the benefits of working with an agency, perhaps you wonder if you or a missionary you know could be an exception. You wonder if—to use an analogy from business sales—"cutting out the middle man" would improve your efficiency and reduce your costs. Instead of working through an agency, perhaps your local church or a friend could help you in ministry.

Let's hear about some of the benefits of working as an independent missionary from those who've done it or know others who have.

Q. Why do some missionaries serve independent of an agency?

A: Because they find help in other ways that costs less in finances and time.

I chose to go the independent route because I felt that I already had (or was able to find) all the services of a mission agency from other sources at a fraction of the cost.

But there are several advantages in being associated with a mission agency, including the following:

- A stamp of legitimacy to help with fundraising;
- Practical help, such as finding health insurance, saving for retirement, receipting donations, setting up housing and transportation for furloughs, and mailing newsletters;
- A structure to guide your ministry efforts, both in the general sense of choosing an assignment and in the short-term sense of month-to-month work;
- Accountability so that you don't fall into sin or into nonproductive activities;
- A team offers encouragement and day-to-day practical help.

If you're fortunate to find a wonderful agency, you will receive all these benefits in some measure.

If you're unfortunate, you'll receive very little but will still have all the disadvantages of working under an agency, including these:

- *Financial cost*. Many mission agencies support their home-office staff from a percentage of the funds raised by overseas missionaries. In addition, your agency may require you to raise more funds than you think you need.
- *Time cost*. Some mission agencies consume an inordinate amount of time with general conferences, field conferences, area meetings, reporting requirements, and other things. I've heard stories of folks losing an entire day each week just in meetings.
- *Relationship cost*. If your agency has others working in your local area, you have to invest the effort to get along

with those folks, even if they have incompatible visions or personalities. You can't choose with whom you work.

- **_Vision cost_**. With an agency, you may have to go along with what they're doing, even if the season for one type of ministry in your area is finished and you feel led to do something different. In most cases, you will have to plug into the vision of your agency's founder or current head, or that of your local team leader, rather than going with the vision God gives you.

My feeling is that all the benefits of a mission agency can be gained in a variety of ways for a fraction of the financial, time, relationship, and vision costs.

In my view, many missionaries are unsuccessful or unproductive for at least one of the following reasons:

- They are not disciplined and self-motivated.
- They don't have a clear vision of what God is leading them to do.
- They are not committed to accountable relationships.

Without these traits you will fail, whether as an independent missionary or as an agency-affiliated missionary. Going with an agency will not make up for these shortcomings.

If you can't honestly say that you are disciplined, have a clear vision, and are committed to accountability, I'd suggest that you pray and fast, review your guidance into missions, and spend a year or two with an "open" agency that emphasizes training and formation of leaders, such as Operation Mobilization or Youth With A Mission. Only after you're certain you have some measure of these traits in your life should you even consider career missions.

Answer from Jay, an independent missionary who has been working in Italy for five years.

A: Because their church serves as a sending agency.

I think missionaries should either choose a mission agency or have their church serve as a sending agency of sorts. In my relatively short time in Japan, most of those here as independents came initially with a mission, but they quit when they had struggles with the leadership or couldn't raise their financial support. Independents often do not fare well under leadership, becoming poor partners with other missionaries and national leadership. Bottom line: most people, especially those first starting out, need to be accountable to someone—either their home church or an agency.

Answer from John, who has served in Japan for five years.

SALARY OR SUPPORT?

Prospective missionaries have many difficult questions to consider, and this certainly is one of them. After all, finances are vital for God's work and our survival. Yet while it would be nice if every door were thrown wide open, God allows obstacles to build us and teach us who he is (in this case, he's our faithful provider).

An open heart will sure make these decisions easier. We do our part to gather information on options, we keep our mind open to the Holy Spirit, and then we go with the guidance God gives. Let's listen in as these missionaries, now looking back, can testify that God does say, "This is the way; walk in it" (Isaiah 30:21).

Q: ■ Should I go with my denomination, which provides a salary, or with a nondenominational agency and raise my support?

A: ■ Consider the advantages of both.

Before joining your denomination's missionary force, ask yourself these preliminary questions: Am I happy with the work my denomination is doing? Am I happy with their policies and their history? Is my denomination serving in areas or geographical situations where God is leading me?

If your answers to the questions above are positive, then consider the following advantages of being sent as a missionary under your denominational board:

- You're familiar with their theology, traditions, and methods.
- You may not have to raise support, since denominations usually have a mission budget, so if they accept you, they will support you.
- You have a ready-made support system in the churches that make up the denomination.
- You'll feel more a part of your home church.
- You'll have an influence in your denomination as the years go by.

You may, however, be unhappy with your denomination's mission work, policies, or history. Or your denomination may not work in the area where God is leading you, yet you feel led to serve God as a missionary. Then you might want to explore a nondenominational agency. However, don't leap too quickly. Take time to explore.

When we were ready to go abroad, we were not happy with the theological orientation of our denomination, even though I had served as a minister within this denomination and had attended one of its seminaries. God led us to a nondenominational mission agency. We had to raise support, which by God's grace we did. Most of our support came from churches within our denomination. Our experience has been a happy one, but so was that of my parents, who served within the denomination.

Answer from Jack Voelkel.

A: Don't let fear of raising support make your decision for you.

The easy answer is to go for a salary with your denominational agency so you "don't have to beg for money." But that is a wrong reason. Raising support is hard, no doubt. But raising your own support has some real advantages that you may not have if your funding comes automatically from a denomination:

- You learn to share your vision in a way that is compelling and inviting to others. It's important to do this, since there will come many times in your missionary service when you wonder why you're there. Being firm in your vision is important.
- You realize in a tangible way that you cannot do this on your own. You see how God provides, which is an important lesson to learn and to live once on the field.
- Many missionaries on denominational salary do not make the effort to build a solid prayer-support team. We were so thankful for the hundreds of people we had praying for us—people we probably never would have met if not for our support-raising efforts.

Effective denominational agencies connect individual missionaries to individual local churches for partnership and prayer support.

Answer from Jim, who has served with The Mission Society for ten years in Kazakhstan.

A: Ask God for his specific plan for you.

When I was preparing to join WEC International, I was approached by a denomination that offered full support if I would join them. Doctrinally we were in harmony, and it seemed ideal. However, the denomination did not work where the Lord was leading my wife and me. About the same time, a church contacted us and said that if we would work with them for two years in our own country, then they would pay our total support while overseas. That was also exciting. But as we prayed, we felt the Lord leading us to decline both offers and join WEC *immediately*.

We did join WEC, and God quickly provided funding for us in the short time we spent visiting friends and churches. When we got to Africa, God arranged in Guinea-Bissau for us to be the first missionaries to enter the Muslim half of the country where we worked with the blessing of the Muslim governor. Six months later, the entire political situation changed. If we had not already been there, we would not have been allowed to enter that part of the country. So if we had taken the generous offer from the church, we might have missed a wonderful open door.

God has a particular plan for you, and he wants you to trust him (Psalm 32:8–9) to reveal that plan. Though I serve with a nondenominational agency, I'm on the mission committee of a denominational church, and I encourage members to serve with the denomination even as I recruit for WEC. I see full validity for both. Ask those who know you for input and pray for guidance.

Answer from David Smith, director of mobilization with WEC International. David has been a missionary for twenty-five years as a field worker in West Africa and at WEC USA headquarters.

Editor's Note: Certain denominations partner with agencies. It's worth checking to see if you can work with both your denomination and an agency.

A THOROUGH EXAM

In some ways, joining an agency is like finding a spouse. It's not quite "until death do we part," though it may feel that way at times. That's why we take the time *before joining* to thoroughly research an agency.

If your home church is part of a denomination, discuss with church and mission leaders whether your denomination's mission department may be a match for you.

If your denominational mission department is not a fit for you, ask your church leaders for a list of sending agencies they would recommend that you research.

Whether you look inside your denomination or at a nondenominational mission agency, ask the penetrating and enlightening questions given in this section. Then discuss your findings, both positive and negative, with a leader in your local church.

Q: How do I select an agency?

A: Look for a fit.

How you choose an agency depends on a variety of factors, including the following:

- Where you desire to serve;
- What you desire to do;
- What your "essential" doctrinal positions are;

- How much input you have in your assignments;
- What your home church thinks of the agency;
- How much support you're required to raise and what percentage goes to the home office;
- The agency's view of the family—for example, how your children will be educated, how much time a married couple spend away from each other, and what happens in case of family difficulties;
- Where, how, and for how long you would receive language training.

If possible, speak to missionaries who work in the organization you're thinking about joining and in the area you're considering. They can give the most accurate perspective of both the positives and the negatives of the organization.

Answer from John, who has served in Japan for five years.

A: Be thorough and ask questions.

In the process of selecting and joining a mission agency, be thorough in your research and ask the following questions:

1. Review the agency's theological orientation.
2. What is their passion? Do they have a unifying focus to their work? If so, what is it?
3. How does the agency work with the local church in sending and caring for missionaries?
4. Who makes the decisions? Are the leaders open to new ideas?
5. What is the organization's vision for the next five years?
6. How are missionaries supervised? Do missionaries have to submit reports? Are reports read?
7. How does the mission avoid paternalism? How do they maintain their vision while listening to and developing national leaders?

Does the mission have plans to move nationals into positions of authority?

Is the mission developing institutions and entities that can be supported nationally?

Are national leaders expected to just carry on the pattern the missionaries have established, or are they expected to lead with their own vision? Are they empowered to do so?

8. How does the agency work with other denominations, ministries, mission organizations, and others in the mission setting?

9. What are their philosophies on and approach to member care and crisis management?

10. What provision is made for missionaries' children? How and where are they to be educated?

11. What orientation is given to missionaries before they go to their place of service? What counsel and support are given when they return to their home country?

12. What provision is made for missionaries' continuing education? Are study leaves encouraged?

13. How much language preparation does the agency allow the missionary candidate to have?

14. What does the organization say are its weaknesses? (This gives insight into their openness toward change and whether they have a healthy self-awareness in a need for growth.)

Don't forget the local church. From the beginning of your selection process, seek leadership and counsel from your local church and pastor. Set up times to regularly meet, pray, and discuss the process with your church's leadership.

Answer from Jack Voelkel.

Editor's Note: Support from your local church is very important, but if you find yourself in a congregation that isn't missions minded, don't be discouraged. Seek a friend or someone from a mission agency to mentor you through this process, and perhaps God will use you to raise missions awareness in your church.

A: Get perspective and ask questions.

When considering a mission agency, it's important to remember that at least four parties have roles in this decision—you, God, the agency, and the church.

First, you can learn what God is doing in the world by taking a mission course such as Perspectives on the World Christian Movement (see "Resources for Further Study"). It will be difficult for you to do your part in making a decision on an agency without embracing the big picture of what God is doing in the world and without being equipped with his promises in the Word. Before we can know his will, we must be committed to doing it and to discovering his total plan for the world. This plan goes beyond the particular country or agency where you wish to go.

Next, the agency must select you as well. You will be under their authority in the place where you serve, and you are under their authority in the selection process. The agency must consider how you will fit on one of their teams; therefore, not being accepted usually is not a poor reflection on you.

Last, your home church has a great role in sending you. Do they feel you're ready? Have you met with your pastor to pray about this? Do you wish to be a co-missionary of your church and the agency? What does the church think of the agency you've chosen?

Methodologies of mission organizations have great consequences, which requires your careful consideration. Do they treat the poor as you would treat Christ? Will you be working with unreached peoples? Does the agency address people's physical, spiritual, and emotional needs?

Does the agency make disciples or just evangelize? Are they committed to planting an indigenous church where there is no church? How does the agency care for their missionaries? How do they resolve conflicts?

Answer from Steve Scheller, director of mobilization for Mission: Moving Mountains.

AGENCIES LARGE AND SMALL

Perhaps these long lists of questions to ask an agency seem overwhelming. Right now, let's focus on just one consideration as a starting point—the size of an agency.

Q. Should I join a larger mission agency or a smaller one?

A: Consider several factors.

First, does the agency work in the country where God is leading you to serve? Next, is the agency large enough to give you proper support and leadership on the field and support in your home country? You want an established group that has member-care guidelines in place and is financially responsible. Integrity counts in missions. You want to be affiliated with an agency with a good reputation.

Answer from Rob, who has served for ten years with Operation Mobilization in Spain, in the United States, and on their ships Logos II and Doulos.

A: Look at the advantages of agencies of all sizes, and most of all, find God's fit for you.

I suggest you start by looking not at an organization, but at what, where, or who interests you. For instance, if you're interested in ministering to Muslims, start by looking at organizations that specialize in work with Muslims, such as Frontiers. If you're a nurse, start by looking at organizations involved in medical missions or community development work.

Sure, many good organizations that don't specialize in nursing or Muslims can still put you, your interests, and your expertise to very good kingdom work. But more important than the size of an organization is how it fits with God's plan for you in this season of ministry.

Answer from Paul, who has served for five years with MDat International and shorttermmissions.com.

A: Smaller may be better.

There are so many excellent agencies that it can be hard to know where to start looking. Size is one way to get started narrowing your choices.

Three advantages of a larger agency include the following:

1. They are usually older—more established and mature.
2. They will usually have more opportunities worldwide.
3. They often have regional setups that will connect you with other missionaries once on the field.

Three advantages of a smaller agency include the following:

1. They are usually more personal—you get to know the staff in a more personal way.
2. They can be more flexible in helping you pursue a specific ministry. A larger organization for the sake of efficiency may tend to have molds that you need to fit into.

3. You have more opportunities to affect the way the agency develops. The fact that it is less established can allow for faster adaptation to new realities.

I have huge respect for many of the larger agencies—they do incredible work. Many people do and should serve in them. But as a veteran missionary from a smaller agency, and now on staff, I'll give a plug for smaller agencies. Throughout our years of exploring our role in missions, staff members helped us discover God's plan rather than sending us forms to complete and simply deploying us to a predefined role. Our agency keeps a personal connection with our missionaries from the time they first contact us onward. And we're able to adapt to different situations, rather than having to work with a large number of missionaries only in general categories.

Your ministry goal may help determine whether a smaller or larger agency is best for you.

Answer from Jim, who has served for ten years in Kazakhstan and now the United States. He is with a smaller agency, The Mission Society.

A:  Larger may be better.

Over nine years, I went on short-term mission trips with a small agency and learned much from the agency and its missionaries and leaders. But when the time came for my family and me to serve full-time, I had several concerns about the small agency. I presented these concerns to the head of the agency, and he was happy to address them. His answers, however, were not satisfactory. Then God directed me to consider two larger agencies that filled the needs and addressed my concerns.

First, determine what God is leading you to do. Is there an agency that lines up with that focus, regardless of the agency's size?

Second, interview the agency leaders. Write down your

concerns; then ask questions as if you were applying for a job. Suggest scenarios to see how the agency would handle them. For example, in all my interviews with agencies, I asked about safety. Since my family is going to serve full-time with me, my concern is for their safety. I asked, "If a country should have an uprising, do you have policies and procedures for the missionaries in that country? If so, what are they?" The follow-up question was, "Have you ever had to implement those policies and procedures?" Some smaller agencies do not have policies or procedures for safety.

Finally, you've done your homework and found out the facts. The most important step now is to ask God for wisdom. He will reveal what you need to know for your future. James 1:5 promises, "If any of you lacks wisdom, he should ask God."

Answer from Bill, who recently changed agencies.

A: Focus on the fit, not on the size.

The most important thing to consider in a mission agency is its DNA—its purpose for existence and ethos. You wouldn't work with a strictly medical mission agency if your goal was to do Bible translation. You want an agency that is a good fit for your goals and personality. The agency I work for is a narrowly focused agency in that we have a specific purpose—mobilizing and training missionaries who will reach the unreached by planting and multiplying the local church. Our aim is not starting seminaries or being a medical mission. Regardless of their qualifications, if the aim of those wanting to join us differs from ours, they would not be a good fit.

Answer from Mark, who has served for three years with Heart of God Ministries.

WHEN TO BEGIN?

Which agency you join is a critical decision that affects your placement, training, supervision, and many other vital areas. It's never too early to look at different agencies and begin the process of discovering which organization God may want you to join.

Q: I am years away from finishing my education. When should I start to look at agencies?

A: Go on mission trips with an agency now.

Start investigating possible agencies now. Read their websites to see where they serve and in what sort of ministries they're involved. Try a short-term mission with your agency of choice to see how it would be to work with them. Also, if you can attend an orientation session before you graduate, then you may be able to start support raising at graduation.

Answer from Rob, who has served for ten years with Operation Mobilization in Spain, in the United States, and on their ships Logos II and Doulos.

A: First talk with your church.

This is not an issue for you to deal with alone. The first step is to submit yourself to your church leadership according to Acts 13:1–4.

As you discuss and pray with your local church leaders, the Holy Spirit will direct you, through confirmations and agreement, toward your role in missions. With this direction in focus, you can begin to look for agencies that serve in that way.

Answer from Neal Pirolo, missionary trainer and author of Serving As Senders.

A: Yes. Invite coaching now.

It is good to begin the exploration early. A good mission agency will want to develop a relationship with you, not simply look at a form, give a thumbs up or thumbs down, and then deploy you. During your university years, they can give advice on experiences that can help you prepare. If an agency simply says, "Call us back when you're out," obviously they're not seeking that sort of relationship and are not as likely to walk with you as you explore your future.

The agency we're with first met us when I was a student. We eventually went overseas nine years later! They walked with us through all those years of discerning God's will and exploring options. They gave no pressure, just a genuine desire to help us go where and when God chose.

Answer from Jim, who has served for ten years in Kazakhstan and now in the United States. He is with a smaller agency, The Mission Society.

MY THOUGHTS SO FAR

There are well over one thousand mission agencies—some large, some small. Thinking through your own answers to this chapter's questions will help you decide on the type of agency you'd love to serve with or if serving independently is right for you.

So ask the Holy Spirit to guide you, through God's Word and through prayer. Answer each question in light of what you *currently* understand from God. Then discuss your responses, concerns, and any unanswered questions with a leader or friend in your local church as you explore how you could become a missionary.

What are my thoughts, both positive and negative, on serving under an agency or denomination? On serving as an independent missionary?

_____

_____

_____

What does my home church think about the agencies in which I'm interested? What agencies does my church recommend?

_____

_____

_____

What are my thoughts, both positive and negative, on joining a larger mission agency? On joining a smaller one?

_____

_____

_____

_____

What are my thoughts, both positive and negative, on raising personal support?

_____

_____

_____

For the agencies I'm interested in, how much financial support would I have to raise?

_____

_____

What percentage of support raised goes to the agency's home office?

_____

_____

What are my essential doctrinal positions?

_____

_____

_____

_____

How much input do I want to have in my placement?

_____

_____

_____

I will invite the input of several missionaries and fellow agency-seeking friends by asking the following questions:

"How did you decide whether to serve under an agency or independently?"

_____

_____

_____

"What can I learn from your decision-making process?"

_____

_____

_____

Add other exploratory questions you might have:

_____
_____
_____

What three questions can I ask to help me determine if an agency is a fit for me? (Consider Jack Voelkel's excellent questions under "A Thorough Exam" earlier in this chapter.)

1. _____
_____

2. _____
_____

3. _____
_____

I will learn more about mission organizations in the following two ways (select from opportunities and/or events listed in "Resources for Further Study" at the end of this book):

1. _____
_____

2. _____
_____

TRAINING
Getting It Right

4

A BULLET TRAIN CAN SHOOT THROUGH THE Russian snowfields at 210 kilometers per hour. Now, hours outside of Moscow, the temperature distinction between outside the train and inside is negligible. And while I'm thankful for tundra-resistant, insulated, microfleece-lined gloves, they lack the dexterity to accurately type on a laptop keyboard.

Nevertheless, I opened last week's *Brigada* e-newsletter and scanned the latest evangelism tools available in various languages, a business-as-mission conference scheduled for next month in Baltimore, and information on a new distance-learning option. But what caught my eye was the publisher's wrap-up, entitled "How Tough It Gets: Satanic Attacks":

> As I travel and talk to cross-cultural workers on the front lines, I'm often reminded of the extent to which Satan goes in his effort to thwart outreaches by newly placed international workers. He goes for the jugular vein—whatever that happens to be for the respective single or family. He can attack the kids: their health, their adaptation, their studies, their self-image, their very souls. Sometimes he goes after spouses: their language-learning ability (or hurdles), their commitments, their promises, their self-images as

well. Sometimes he goes after family members back home: ailing parents, unwilling grandparents, doubting "friends," flagging support. And sometimes, in a seeming lack of creativity, he'll boldly challenge our spiritual foundation with doubts: God's existence, salvation, spiritual gifts, our future.[1]

With chilling accuracy, he further expounded on the reality of the principalities, powers, and rulers of darkness in this world. Finally, he asked *Brigada* readers, many who are front-line missionaries, to reply to this question: How can we train for the realities of spiritual warfare in mission work? Peter, the first reader to comment, said it well: "Simply being forewarned can make a huge difference."

That first week in Moscow was itself a forewarning, a loud wake-up call for the need to be trained in handling spiritual attacks. Shirley, my missionary counselor, had guided me station by station through the confusing Moscow train system. All the while, she spoke of routinely encountering Satan's attacks. When the train approached our final station, we pushed our way toward the doorway, through the too-close-for-comfort crowd. The real pressure of the crowd at that moment illustrated with unsettling clarity the also real but unseen pressures satanic forces can apply. Missionaries and the mission fields of the world are particular targets of the enemy of our souls.

Now, one week after my forewarning in Moscow, a different train is finally slowing to a stop in Perm, the largest city in this frozen region. I clearly recall the pressure of demonic forces in a place as civilized as Moscow, which makes me wonder what spiritual oppression might challenge me out here, especially tomorrow, in the prison town of Nyrob. But for now, the crystal-clean air—a balmy minus-25 degrees Celsius—feels thoroughly cleansing, removed from the grungy uneasiness of the dark spirits of Moscow. My second relief comes in the faces of my missionary team, waiting on the platform.

After a treacherous five-hour drive on a snow packed road, my team of two missionary friends and I finally arrived in the countryside village of Nyrob. If ever a forewarning were appropriate, it would seem necessary for this despairing, seemingly hopeless town. But the opposite was true.

Our driver grew increasingly excited driving through the barbed wire fence of Nyrob Prison Sixteen and toward its maximum security building. "Over there's the chapel," he declared. "We're almost finished with the renovations. We had to replace the logs it rests on—sort of its foundation. So we lifted the entire building on a whole set of car jacks. Pretty exciting!"

He slid to a stop near the prison gate and instructed us to "bring the books and Bibles." As we neared the guards, he whispered to us, "Nyrob Sixteen is where repeat offenders of heinous crimes are imprisoned. Some of Russia's worst convicts." My uneasiness returned.

Once inside the gate and through a side door, however, we stepped into the prison's "prayer room." No darkness here, just a bright room decorated with dozens of wooden hand carvings of the cross, the face of Jesus, and open Bibles. Eleven smiling Christian prisoners stood in the little chapel. These men greeted us with bear hugs, all saying, "Come in, brothers!" And they asked, "Can you baptize us this summer?"

Suddenly, loud music rolled into the prayer room from down the hall. With only one guard following us, the eleven prisoners led us to the cafeteria, where one hundred or so rough, scarred faces were waiting. Our brothers set out chairs for us, and our translator scooted near to translate for the seedy soloist strumming at the front of the prisoner band—two electric guitars, a bass, drums, and an acoustic guitar.

"He's singing a song they wrote themselves."

> *I've been set free from my old sin,*
> *My renewed soul now is longing.*
> *After I finish my earthly world,*
> *I want to enter your eternal peace.*

I took it all in. The blaring Soviet-era sound equipment. The music echoing inside the stone walls. Weathered faces and gravelly voices.

Do Satan and his cohorts have a frightening grip on the struggling people of Russia? *Yes!*

Is Jesus Christ bringing release and freedom in a maximum security prison hundreds of miles into the country's frozen expanse? *Yes!*

My missionary training must cover the dark, spiritual realities of God's expanding kingdom beating against the gates of hell. But

I must also rejoice in the amazing breakthroughs Jesus brings. He proclaims freedom for the captives and release from darkness for the prisoners.

And then came the prisoner band's closing verse:

> *Draw me a little house near the spring,*
> *Let it flow in freedom like a tiny stream.*
> *Draw me the cross that I could take it with me,*
> *I've been set free.*

RIGHT FROM THE START

Moving along the path that leads to missionary service, we eventually consider which training options will best prepare us for our role in God's mission. As stewards of our time and resources, we want to get the right training, right from the start.

In this chapter, missionaries address many aspects of preparation. They discuss whether to train before going overseas or whether to get on-the-job training. From their own experiences, they tell us which types of training they recommend. Other discussions include academic options, ways to learn a language, and ways to handle culture shock.

Then, of course, there are all those surprises that now-on-the-field missionaries realize their training didn't cover. In those discussions, missionaries let you in on things they wish they had known *before* they arrived on the field. Let's begin looking at what preparation is right for you.

A **.** Ask God for his specific plan for you.

Satan has always tried to bring a wedge between those in the mission world who strongly emphasize on-the-job training and those who advocate academic training. Surely it's not either/or but both/and. Some people are gifted in learning as they work in missions, while others find this almost impossible and need the discipline that a good academic environment gives.

Let's remember that even those who are highly trained professionals can make huge blunders on the mission field. Because we tend to overreact to a mistake (I know I have), we all too quickly communicate that the mistake would not have happened if the person had more training, or more teaching, or better doctrine, or some other oversimplification.

Over the years, thousands who have worked in OM's short-term program, often for a specific purpose such as working in the engine room on a ship, have later ended up in Bible college or similar training to further prepare for a different ministry. Surely, God leads different people in different ways, just as he uses people in different ways.

Answer from George Verwer, who started Operation Mobilization (OM) and has worked in missions for over fifty years.

A: Persevere, study, and look for learning opportunities.

Remember that the Lord wants to teach us what it means to hear his voice and to help us grow in faith, grace, obedience, and holiness (2 Peter 3:18; Romans 8:29). God wants us to learn to *persevere*. So don't be surprised when you encounter difficulty, personal conflict, and even anxiety. In all of these training opportunities the Lord is teaching you to depend on him.

As you learn to persevere, also be faithful to *study*. Daily read the Bible and pray. If you're not doing it already, include in your prayer time intercession for non-Christian friends and needy areas of the world. *Operation World* is an excellent resource for praying for each country of the world (see "Resources for Further Study"). As you read about these countries, ask the Lord to put places or areas of ministry on your heart. Also, read the daily newspaper through mission eyes. Soon you'll find that certain areas of the world claim greater attention. Research and pray more frequently for those areas.

The following are other *learning opportunities*:

- Take advantage of exposure to mission opportunities through conferences, correspondence with missionaries, and contact with mission agencies.
- Read widely. My favorite genre of literature is biographies. Read Ruth Tucker's book *From Jerusalem to Irian Jaya*, which is a collection of short biographies of missionaries throughout history (see "Resources for Further Study").
- Include in your schedule intentional ministry opportunities. In addition to faithfully worshiping in a local congregation, intentionally share the gospel and help new Christians grow in their walk with the Lord.
- Seriously consider formal Bible training, either full-time or by correspondence. I strongly recommend the Perspectives course, which is offered through the U.S. Center for World Mission (see "Resources for Further

Study"). It will give you a systematic presentation of the biblical theology of mission as well as what's going on in cross-cultural ministry today.

Answer from Jack Voelkel, missionary-in-residence with the Urbana Student Mission Convention. Previously Jack served thirty years with Latin America Mission in Peru and Colombia.

A: Training develops our spirit and our character.

The purpose of training is to strengthen weak areas, to improve attitudes, to provide problem-solving skills, and to hasten spiritual and emotional maturation. Training should improve our learning ability, make us more adaptable and flexible, enable us to trust and appreciate others, and above all, deepen our spiritual life.[2]

Answer from Thomas Hale, who served in Nepal for over twenty years and is now president of International Nepal Fellowship.

TO TRAIN OR NOT TO TRAIN?

Here's a wise statement: "Don't decide too quickly." In wanting to get our preparation right, we must allow God time to shape us however he chooses for our specific role in missions.

Today's missionaries serve cross-culturally in capacities as diverse as teaching in a major urban university and developing a community health program in a village. Whatever your specific role may be, the appropriate training enables you to be a more effective servant of God. So let's slowly consider whether to train or not to train.

Q: Should I skip a degree and go into missions now?

A: Probably not.

Don't decide too quickly to skip getting a degree. It's one thing for the Lord to direct you. It's quite another to drop everything and rush off into ministry. The great majority of effective, cross-cultural missionaries I've met have a solid education that both shaped them as people and trained them for a specific task. You will also want to get some formal Bible and theological training. In the meantime, it's important for you to seek ministry opportunities right where you are.

Answer from Jack Voelkel.

A: Instead of a degree, learn from the Holy Spirit.

I would say that not all people going into ministry need four years of training. We as an agency have seen people go into missions with only basic evangelistic training, and God trains them further while in service. Having said that, some people go to seminary, and God can still use them. But many times he has to deprogram them.

As a missionary for the past thirty years, I've come to rely completely on the Holy Spirit for my wisdom, my counsel to others, and my outreach to the lost. Even though I have Bible school degrees, I find that the best teacher is the Holy Spirit.

Answer from Rocco, who served for thirty years in South Africa, Nigeria, and Mexico.

A: Fast can end up being slow.

A degree may or may not be what you need. It really depends on what your passions are and what contribution you hope to make in the long term. For example, if you want to be an advocate for the poor, you need to learn the laws that govern the poor, and you need to gain a position from which your voice can be heard.

There are many types of good and relevant training in our world today, and a formal degree may be very beneficial—or it may not be—depending on where you want to go and what type of service you want to be to the people among whom you will live. The bottom line is that we need to be trained, mentored, discipled, and developed. We first need to develop the spiritual disciplines so that we can truly know and follow Christ ourselves—showing by example how others can know and follow Christ. Second, we will be of greater assistance to communities and people if we improve our God-given talents.

Remember: fast can be slow. Taking shortcuts may hinder you from realizing your greatest vision. On our journey with God, we gain the wisdom, faith, strength, skills, character, and courage to reach the goal. Those who take shortcuts often fall out of the race because they did not have what they needed to finish.

Answer from Lisa, who has served for fifteen years in Austria, Romania, and Canada with International Teams.

A: Prepare as much as possible; then go.

We all have much to learn in this life, and much of what God has to teach we learn only by going where he leads. So do some thorough preparation, and then GO. Don't ever think you have to be totally prepared before you go—or you will never go.

Answer from Tim, who has served in Cameroon and in the United States with Wycliffe Bible Translators for twenty-five years.

Q. Can Christians without advanced training be involved in missions?

A: Yes.

Maybe you don't have a degree, but there's probably something you know a lot about and that you do well, whether it's motorcycle repair or worship music or serving. Whatever it is, God has put those specific tools into your hands to use for his glory among the nations. With a little knocking on doors, you can find a niche somewhere in world missions for anything you're good at. One warning, though: you shouldn't become a missionary unless you're willing to learn new things in the process!

Answer from Nate Wilson, mission mobilizer with Caleb Project.

A: No matter your role, some training is necessary.

If you're thinking of working in missions, you should first look for an agency to send you. All agencies have requirements, which may include educational preferences. Missionaries do many things today; not all are preachers or teachers. All should be prepared, however, as Peter tells us (1 Peter 3:15), to "give an answer to everyone who asks you to give the reason for the hope that you have," whether working as a physician, agronomist, or mechanic.

Our ministry, wherever we are, should be holistic. The proper perspective would be to decide what the Lord is leading you to be and do, and then, as much as possible, to fully prepare. If you get formal training, make sure you include some courses in cross-cultural communication.

Answer from Jack Voelkel.

Q: I am in my late teens. Should I take some missionary training now, before I go to college?

A: No. Do university studies now and short-term trips during breaks.

If by going to missionary training you might lose motivation to go to college, then go directly to college. College is foundational. Although it's sometimes hard to spend four or more years in school when you'd rather be on the field, persevere.

Take advantage of ministry opportunities both now and throughout any training you receive. I taught English to an Indonesian student a few hours a week while I was in college, and many schools offer short-term mission trips during spring and summer breaks.

Learn a variety of things you're interested in. One friend used cosmetology to pay for college and will probably use it overseas. I taught piano to help pay for college and now find that teaching opens opportunities for ministry.

Christian campus groups at secular universities are a great place to pick up evangelism training and practice.

Also, if you're narrowing down what agency you want to work

with, check their education preferences. Don't lose time just because you failed to ask their requirements.

Answer from Bethany, who is serving in the Middle East with the Assemblies of God.

A: Yes. Take a year or two for missions before college.

My friends and relatives were pretty jumpy at the thought of me doing a year or two of mission work before getting into college. Maybe more than anyone else, I was afraid of taking a road less traveled. Was it really the right choice? I was worried that I would eventually go back home to start college and be a "missionary misfit." I would be a few years older than my classmates, with a different worldview, experiences, and morals that would set me apart in an awkward way. But at the same time, I knew that my foundation as a Christian had been strengthened and that I would be more prepared to face the world with a better understanding of myself.

Now that I have finished my two years of missionary service and have been in college, I find that I am not a misfit after all. I actually feel better prepared to disciple and encourage my brothers and sisters in Christ because of my experiences, and I find myself recruiting my friends into missions. Everyone, whether Christian or not, enjoys hearing my missionary stories. The fact that I am a few years older than my classmates has actually turned out to be a blessing.

There is a place and a time for university, but a year or two off will undoubtedly teach you more about who you are, who God is, and how you can actively serve in God's kingdom.[3]

Answer from Hannah, who trained and served for two years with Operation Mobilization.

A$\begin{smallmatrix} \blacksquare \\ \blacksquare \end{smallmatrix}$ In the middle of your university education, take a year off for missions.

My first mission trip was a summer in Asia while still in high school. Then after my first year at college, I spent ten weeks in East Africa. I received firsthand experience in missions, and now I know it's where I want to be.

This year I'm taking a one-year hiatus from university studies to serve aboard a Mercy Ship in West Africa. I think taking missionary training before going to school is important, if you already know you want to be a missionary. If you can, take some mission trips to a few different places to make sure God has led you into missions and to get an idea of where you would want to be in the world.

Answer from Mark in Tulsa, who took a year off for missions after his first year of college.

Q$\begin{smallmatrix} \blacksquare \\ \blacksquare \end{smallmatrix}$ **Does the spouse of a missionary also need formal Bible training?**

A$\begin{smallmatrix} \blacksquare \\ \blacksquare \end{smallmatrix}$ Yes. Just study through a correspondence course thirty minutes a day, three times a week, for one or two years.

You will need some courses to prepare for mission service, but it's not impossible to do. A number of Bible colleges have one or two levels of correspondence courses. One level gives college credit, along with the appropriate cost and amount of work. The other level, designed for lay people, is inexpensive, and while good, is not as in-depth. WEC accepts a number of these as fulfillment of a required Bible class.

Why are there training requirements at all? History at WEC and a number of other agencies has shown that spouses of missionaries will have many ministry opportunities overseas, whether they seek them or not. Your home will be a place of friendship and hospitality. People will come to you. History also shows that spouses who do not feel adequately prepared become discouraged and begin wanting to come home, which most eventually do.

Correspondence courses have helped many spouses feel prepared. Therefore, I encourage you to examine several correspondence courses and begin studying one or two, knowing it will take time and discipline.

Answer from David Smith, director of mobilization with WEC International. David has been a missionary for twenty-five years as a field worker in West Africa and at WEC USA headquarters.

A: No formal Bible training is required.

Our agency does not require a formal Bible degree for the missionary spouse. My wife and I served in Mexico for seventeen years. She has no formal training yet ministered to our family and to Mexican women. She related to them as a mother and a wife, not as a formally educated minister.

I honestly believe that she had more success in ministry coming as a mother and wife. We team-taught marriage courses and worked in churches together. She was and still is priceless to our work.

Answer from Dale Pugh, international coordinator of World International Mission, who served long term in Mexico.

AVENUES OF TRAINING

Learning should be lifelong. Even Jesus—the Word who attended his Father at creation (John 1)—grew in wisdom and in stature. So should we.

The avenues of training discussed in this section are Bible school, correspondence courses, university, graduate school, and practical ministry experience. Each has value, as we discover from several missionaries who offer their wisdom and experience in these avenues.

Q: **What types of training do experienced missionaries promote?**

A: Look into these five options for training.

Match the educational mode to your needs, goals, resources, personality, and learning style. Here are five options:

- Secular colleges and universities,
- Christian liberal arts colleges and universities,
- Bible colleges,
- Correspondence study with World Christian Foundations (see "Resources for Further Study"),
- Christian graduate schools and seminaries.

Whatever avenue of training or study you choose, it can be a rich phase of your life. It's a time when lifelong friends are made and life partners are often found. Surrounded by like-minded teachers and students, you'll find freedom and support to test your calling and refine the direction of your life.[4]

Answer from Steve Hoke and Bill Taylor, veteran missionaries who also grew up on the mission field.

A: Study at a Bible college first.

Before I came to Estonia, I attended a two-year Bible college. Ten years before that, I graduated from university with a bachelor of science degree in mechanical engineering. If I had to do it over again, I would go to a Bible college first, then to university. At Bible college, I learned crucial things about believing God and following the Holy Spirit. I can't imagine that I would be doing what I'm doing if I had not gone to Bible college. The things we learn at Bible college can make us more successful at whatever we do.

Answer from Tom, who has been a missionary in Estonia for six years.

A: Study at a Christian university.

A traditional university degree, along with the necessary Bible skills, is probably the best way to go. Many good Christian colleges offer both. To focus solely on missions may cause us to miss an important skill. On the other hand, to miss ministry and Bible training may stifle our knowledge on how to most effectively serve the Lord in missions.

Answer from Glen, who has been a missionary among Russian-speaking people for seven years.

A: Get experience in your church, and study through a correspondence course.

I have been to a state school, a Christian school, and a liberal arts theological school. However, the best education that I've had is not from a traditional educational institution.

I've found that regularly participating in the church and its outreach efforts is essential. A good hour or more each day in prayer and Bible reading has also proven profitable. Small groups are another key way to grow.

As for a training curriculum, the best education I've received has been through World Christian Foundations from William Carey International University (see "Resources for Further Study"). It's largely a correspondence school with the benefit of a local face-to-face mentor and then the opportunity to apply the training by teaching someone else.

This method has enabled me to remain active in the community and to learn from a thoroughly mission-oriented curriculum. Think creatively about learning, and remember that the goal is service, not academic credentials.

Answer from Mert, who has helped pastor a small church and has a masters degree in biblical studies / languages. Mert is currently pursuing a second masters degree by correspondence.

A: I attended Bible school, even though I could not read well.

Once my first short-term mission trip was over, I thought, *If God is leading me in this direction, I need some training.* My first step was to attend a discipleship training school. This involved six months of training, with one month in Mexico working among the local churches. I figured that if I were truly going to work overseas, I should get some preparation. Everyone I knew who served God overseas was, in my eyes, a highly educated person—with an undergraduate and graduate degree in theology, medicine, or education. I had struggled with my academic inabilities in high school. How could God use someone like me to serve in another country? I could not read well, I was not a good speaker, I hated being in front of a class, and I preferred to be last rather than first to answer a question. I decided to test the waters. I would apply to Bible school, and if they did not accept me, I would know it wasn't God's will. But surprisingly, they did accept me.

The classes at Bible school were just what I needed. I found a new fascination for the Old Testament. The mission and evangelism classes were challenging and demanding with all the memorization, but later I realized how valuable those Scripture passages were to my daily life. The doctrine classes were revealing as I learned about the different doctrinal beliefs. At school, we had the opportunity to not only study and work on the campus but also to take part in outreach ministries. All these areas shaped my life more than I could imagine. It is one thing to know God's Word; it's another to live it and to explain God's truths to others who have never heard them. That was twenty years ago. Those preparation years at discipleship training school, Bible school, my year of internship, and then my hands-on training on the field were life changing.[5]

Answer from Ruth, who has been a missionary in South Asia with Operation Mobilization for twenty years.

A: Get some training now, on furlough, or both.

Anyone who ventures into cross-cultural missions without some kind of preparation is nuts. One can be self-taught to some extent through selected reading, but usually one will need to go through a training orientation program, and in some cases attend a Bible college. No one should begrudge the time spent in such preparation. It will cut out half the stress of arrival on the field, keep one from making needless mistakes, and make one a much better missionary.

How much training should you get in your chosen field? If you are sure you are going to need a particular level of training, then it's best to get it before you go. However, if you are uncertain, then such training is better postponed until your first furlough, or even later. You will usually benefit more from the training once you have been on the field and seen the needs firsthand.[6]

Answer from Thomas Hale, who served in Nepal for over twenty years and is now president of International Nepal Fellowship.

Q: I have years of schooling left. How do I prepare and persevere?

A: Learn about missions and participate in mission-related ministries now.

I was in my midteens when I felt God leading me into missions, so as a teenager I took short-term mission trips. I also became involved in church work with an ethnic group (Hispanic) different from my own. This gave me more insight into other cultures, helped to solidify my direction, and equipped me for the future.

Take every opportunity you can to find out more about missions. Read mission magazines to learn about current mission activities around the world. Read biographies about missionaries. Talk to missionaries when you can. Find out more about missions by attending a Perspectives on the World Christian Movement course (see "Resources for Further Study"). Continue to take any step you believe will help your goal to become a missionary. Avoid choices that might prevent you from going to the mission field, such as incurring large debt or marrying someone not interested in missions.

If possible, find someone to mentor you and pray for you during the years of preparation to become a missionary. There may be many years before you move overseas, but God is faithful to help you get there—if you persevere.

Answer from Mike, who served for ten years in West Africa and North Africa on a Bible translation team with WEC International.

A: Go, learn, befriend, read, and serve.

Go on as many different short-term trips as possible, preferably those that bring you into contact with long-term missionaries. There is no better way to learn than to sit at their feet.

Learn a second language. Learn Spanish if you have a heart for Latin America, French if you have a heart for Africa, and so on. If there is a community college in your area that offers a course in a different language family than your mother tongue, take classes to try it out and hone your language-learning ability.

Make friends with international students in your school and community.

Read, read, read. There is much to be learned from reading missionary biographies. Be inspired by their perseverance through every kind of trial, despite seeing little fruit for many years. Check out Mary Slessor, Hudson Taylor, Jim Elliot, William Carey, St. Patrick, and Adoniram Judson. Use the missionary biography series by Janet and Geoff Benge, *Christian Heroes: Then and Now* (see "Resources for Further Study").

Stay in the Word and prayer and look for an opportunity to minister in your own church. It doesn't have to be related to missions. Just start trying things and thereby discover and confirm your spiritual gifts. Get experience in loving the unlovable and reaching those who don't know they need to be reached.

Answer from Keri, who served in China for four years.

A: Volunteer, integrate faith into your studies, and seek direction.

Here are three in-the-meantime ways to prepare and train for missionary service:

1. ***Volunteer***. Take advantage of different opportunities to work with others in order to learn more about your gifts and interests as well as to practice what you're learning. This may include involvement in a church—a Sunday school class or youth group. Participate in a campus Christian fellowship. Look for options to work with inner-city kids, whether with a Christian organization or not. Be willing to push beyond your comfort zone.

2. ***Integrate***. At the end of every preparatory course you take, write a page or two on "What did I learn in this course that will help me serve later?" Then apply the basic principles to the needs of others.

   Also, work on integrating the scientific principles you're learning with the spiritual principles the Lord is teaching you through your Bible reading, sermons you hear, conversations with mature Christians, and books you read. This will be a challenge. Look for appropriate opportunities to work Christian principles into your academic papers, even though your professors may question you. Make sure you quote respected Christian sources. Don't be discouraged if you're criticized or even ridiculed. Be willing to be stretched, but don't be obnoxious.

3. ***Seek***. Ask the Lord to lay a country or a mission on your heart through reading, meeting a missionary, or attending a missionary conference. Get to know one or two missionaries who impress you, ask to receive their prayer letters, and intercede for them faithfully. Go on mission trips. Bombard visiting missionaries you respect with questions, the harder the better. The time will come when you begin receiving

from the Lord a specific focus, a burden, and a desire.

Answer from Jack Voelkel.

ACADEMICALLY SPEAKING

One hundred years ago, most missionaries served in rural areas, where the skills needed to survive topped the list of mission-necessary training. We've come a long way. Today's missionaries may have academic training in humanities, English, computer technology, or theology. And while survival skills are no longer critical, experienced missionaries add into this section's discussion their suggestions on the academic credentials helpful for working in a restricted-access nation.

With so much to consider, the academic options are endless. Let's consider, however, from the wisdom of those who've seen years of service, how God may be leading you to prepare academically for your role in his mission.

Q. What major in university would be most helpful for missions?

A. Consider a degree in teaching, business, or humanities.

If you're looking into serving in a creative- or limited-access country or a closed country, a degree in teaching English as a second language is useful. Or a degree in computer technology is useful, especially if it puts you into a teaching or entrepreneurial capacity. If you're looking into serving in a more open country as a traditional missionary, then anthropology or any degree in teaching can be quite helpful.

For someone eager to become a missionary, my agency can work with almost any university degree, including history, psychology, philosophy, and business. If you're studying at a secular school, then get involved with Christian campus groups and receive valuable ministry training.

Finally, I recommend taking a language at university. If you can take one language for four years, wonderful; two languages for two years each, almost as wonderful; or one language for two years, still good. You may never use that particular language overseas, but the practice of learning another language will assist you in whatever language you later will need to learn.

Answer from David Smith, director of mobilization with WEC International. David has been a missionary for twenty-five years as a field worker in West Africa and at WEC USA headquarters.

A: Get broadly trained in a field that interests you.

Here are three considerations to keep in mind as you evaluate the choice of a major:

1. University prepares a person more for life than for a job, though it does help to orient and guide toward a job. So a helpful background for ministry or missions would be in the humanities, probably as broad a selection as possible. Fields such as history, literature, psychology, anthropology (especially cultural anthropology), and perhaps even sociology prepare you to understand people, their culture, and their basic ideas and needs. If you plan to attend graduate school, I highly encourage you to pick a major in one of the

above fields, take the minimum courses required in that major, and then take electives in the other fields listed above.

2. A second consideration has to do with you as a person. Exploring your interests in depth may prepare you well for the unique place of ministry for which God has made you and is preparing you.

3. A third, and often neglected, aspect of preparation has to do not so much with a major as with exposure. I urge you to make friends with people who are different from you (other races, other cultures), participate in a mission trip, and get involved in ministry on campus. Learn how to develop your own spiritual life, how to share the gospel, how to answer the tough questions, and how to help a new Christian grow. These are skills you'll use all your life, and there is no better place to learn them than right where you are. I encourage you to move into the dorms or some other incarnational evangelism position, where you live with people whom you might not have chosen to be your friends.

Answer from Jack Voelkel.

Q. Should I get a secular degree to work in a closed country?

A. Don't be afraid of having a Bible-based education.

I went to a Christian university and now live in a Muslim-majority country. I'm thankful for the Bible-based, general education classes that help me integrate my training in social work into my ministry now.

If you will work in a sensitive country, many universities will work with you to creatively rename your major. Some Christian universities will issue a transcript or diploma giving a generic name, such as "International University," which avoids problems in restricted-access nations.

Answer from Bethany, who is serving in the Middle East with the Assemblies of God.

Q: Should I pursue a graduate degree in my profession or stop at a bachelor's degree?

A: It depends on the work you'll do and the context of that work.

Many variables are involved here. Much will depend on the agency with which you go (if you plan to go with one) and on their requirements. Also, consider the type of work you anticipate doing, whether it's practical, hands-on work or teaching at a university. In addition, consider the country where you'll be and its level of development.

I suggest at least two or three years at a Bible school or theological seminary, with a focus on cross-cultural communication. It's one thing to know principles of your profession. It's quite another to know how to get those principles across in a context totally foreign to you, because you will undoubtedly encounter people who find it difficult to receive ideas from an "expert" from another country.

If you plan to teach in a recognized institution, you'll undoubtedly want a higher level of training. But the people in the local situation should advise you on the details. In my own case, I'm glad that

I did my postgraduate study after my first term on the field. I had the language, knew the situation, and was aware of what I needed, which guided my choice of both subject and place to study.

Answer from Jack Voelkel.

A: Get all the training you can get—if it's practical training.

Practical training is critical. As a medical doctor, I use everything I have ever learned. But not everyone needs a doctorate. I know of a very devoted man who got a master's degree in international development. His master's has proven to be nearly useless. He works here in Honduras with the very poor, helping them adopt better farming methods. He does not come from an agricultural background, and he spent only four months at a training site learning agricultural methods. With little practical training, he's been here for twelve years with little to show for it.

Answer from David, a physician internist who has served for eight years in Honduras. David coordinates the medical aspects of several community development groups.

A: A graduate degree can open doors overseas.

I encourage you to continue with graduate studies. Graduate degrees are highly respected and may open doors of opportunity that a bachelor's degree will not. You're far more likely to receive visa approval with a graduate degree, especially a degree in a secular field, than with a bachelor's degree.

I know it can seem like a waste of precious time. But while you're in graduate school, you have the time to further develop your plans for where and with what organization you will serve. It also allows you to "friend raise" as you share with others the ultimate purpose behind your studies. The time spent getting a graduate degree is a perfect opportunity to better prepare for all God has planned for your exciting future.

Answer from Ric, serving with Open Doors in Tulsa.

Q: What training for missions should I get to serve people with special needs?

A: Consider social work.

There are endless skills needed to work with people in crisis — but one person doesn't need to have them all.

Everyone working in a social field should study basic areas as well as areas of specific interest and expertise to bring into a project. You do need to understand trauma issues and its impact on children developmentally, socially (including discipline, attachment, boundaries), spiritually, intellectually, and emotionally.

A degree in social work (at least in most programs I know) is better suited to trauma care than are psychological programs. It's hard to define, but the Western psychological approaches generally aren't helpful for crisis care. They rely on formal methods of measurement and testing. Trauma care, however, depends more on observation, such as studying a child's play and emotional responses. Counseling courses can be helpful. Social work should also give you the skills needed for project development. In any program, there are three aspects of need to address: children, projects, and caregivers. Caregivers often need care too, due to the stresses and demands of crisis care.

Other areas of expertise that are needed in social projects, according to your interest and ability, could include vocational training skills, sports and play therapies, nonformal education, medicine, or music therapy.

Answer from Phyllis Kilbourn, founder of Rainbows of Hope and Crisis Care Training International.

Q: Why is God training me in a way that doesn't make sense?

A: Because his ways are higher than our ways.

I've found that with a willingness to serve, God often finds wonderful ways to prepare us for what lies ahead. Often, our idea of direction undergoes modification. That is, many times the preparations we made when we were willing turn out to be the *exact* preparations needed for the vision that overtakes us as we follow his leading. And sometimes the task that we take on in our willingness turns out to be a better preparation than the task we would have chosen.

Think on this insightful verse, found in Exodus 13:17: "When Pharaoh let the people go, God did not lead them on the road through the Philistine country, though that was shorter."

Answer from John Crouch MD, executive director of In His Image Medical Missions.

A: God's plan for us in missions isn't limited to our education.

I once heard Elisabeth Elliot say at an Urbana Student Missions Conference, "Never let your education stand in the way of the will of God." This is a startling statement for so many young people who often assume their education is or will be the primary avenue of future ministry.

The Spirit has wired you with a particular set of spiritual gifts as well as given you a specific call that matches your ministry burden and passion. Your undergraduate degree and even graduate work in hand may contribute to that calling. But do not hesitate if you sense the Spirit leading you into a role that does not depend on your previous education. Go with the Spirit.

From my experience, about 60 percent of those who end up in missions can utilize their undergraduate major and degree. Others find that the Spirit is directing them into a new arena of outreach, where they lead out of their giftings rather than their competence and learned skills. Listening to God is the best way to remain in alignment with the often surprising leading of the Spirit.

Answer from Steve Hoke, veteran missionary trainer and co-author of Global Mission Handbook *(see "Resources for Further Study").*

LET'S TALK ABOUT LANGUAGE

Once we've determined, through counsel and prayer, the training avenues and academics that best fit us, language learning is our next big consideration. Admittedly, some of us would rather skip this part of mission training, especially if our previous experiences in learning a language were frustrating.

But consider Philippians 2:13, as written in the *Amplified Bible*:

"[Not in your own strength] for it is God Who is all the while effectually at work in you [energizing and creating in you the power and desire], both to will and to work for His good pleasure and satisfaction and delight."

Even when our will prefers something other than God's will, he can create within us the energy *and the desire* to do what he asks. He can match our will to his so that we gain the strength, the power, and the desire to dig into the task, in this case language learning.

Following God is exciting stuff. For further insight or motivation, let's read on.

 Q: ▪ Can I become a missionary if ▪ I don't want to learn another language?

A: ▪ Yes.

Yes, you can be a missionary to some group where at least some people speak your language. Many from unreached people groups are moving to other areas or countries where they learn to speak English. Frequently, when resistant people move elsewhere, they become open to the gospel. In addition, many working with international business companies speak English, so you have vast opportunities with educated middle- and upper-class people. Finally, worldwide over 400 million people speak English.

Also consider the global market for you as an English teacher.

If you're a native English speaker, you could go just about anywhere in the world to teach or tutor English. Language doesn't need to be a barrier. Visit ESL-jobs.com, a website that mobilizes Christians to take jobs teaching English as a second language in Asia. These are ministry positions, but they also offer some income.

Finally, examine your heart concerning the language issue. Are you unwilling to try to learn at least some of a foreign language? You should do some language learning to show the love of Christ wherever you go.

Answer compiled from submissions from missionaries Moisés, Ken, Jim, and Nate.

A: Speaking the language is critical to making disciples.

Throughout our organization, we stress the need to learn the language and understand the culture of the people among whom we live. Our experiences have convinced us that these things become critically important to the effectiveness of making disciples. People have to hear and understand the gospel both in word and in deed.

If you're unwilling to learn another language, then I would definitely advise you to work only among those who speak a language common to you both.

In any case, I encourage you to ask the Lord to bring you freedom to fulfill his purposes. Honestly express your fears to God. If learning another language would best fulfill his purposes for you, then start praying for a transformation in your heart and mind and for the grace and courage to take up the challenge.

Answer from Lisa, who has served fifteen years in Austria, Romania, and Canada with International Teams.

A: Language learning may be easier than you think.

To learn another language, our agency has new missionaries go to Southeast Asia to live with a local family. After four months of language study, some start leading simple Bible studies. Most don't study the language longer than twelve months. I acknowledge that some languages are harder to learn than others. But it's well worth being able to communicate on the heart level in the local language. Whether or not you achieve fluency, every effort toward learning the language will put you ahead in relating to people.

Answer from Jim, who served twenty-five years in Asia with The Navigators.

Q: What is the best way for me to learn a language so I can witness?

A: Go to language school and practice in the culture.

The normal pattern for those of us working in other cultures is to go through the hard slogging of learning another language. It's a lot of work and takes a lot of time, but it has significant benefits. As we work through a language, we learn both intellectual suppositions and cultural niceties of those with whom we desire to communicate the gospel.

A language school addresses both the language and the culture and usually provides a disciplined time frame—something most of us need. Many of us feel it is false economy to rush too quickly into ministry opportunities before receiving an ample grounding in the language we'll be working in. (Also, some of us take longer than others to become adequately fluent!)

Answer from Jack Voelkel.

A: The best way to learn a language depends on the language and on your learning style.

The right method for learning a new language depends on two key factors.

First, it depends on the nature of the language. For example, Spanish is not nearly as difficult to learn as some other widely spoken languages. Because Spanish is easier, many learners can make considerable progress using tutors, language helpers, or even LAMP (Language Acquisition Made Practical). But other learners beware: do not treat all languages the same. Not all languages are easy to learn, and anyone who advocates one method for all the languages spoken on earth is failing to understand the differences between languages.

Second, consider your individual personality and natural ability to learn. The approach you choose should also take into consideration your learning style, which usually has to do with how your mind processes new information. Understanding whether you are an auditory, visual, or perhaps an analytical learner is a plus. Similarly, and more important, your ability to learn a foreign language (expressed as *language aptitude*) must also be taken into account. I recommend that you take a good language aptitude assessment in order to understand how you learn languages.

Answer from Marc, who has served sixteen years in Russia and Ukraine with the Institute of Strategic Languages and Cultures.

A: Learn from a language helper.

Many people still advocate using the Language Acquisition Made Practical (LAMP) method, which majors on memorizing useful phrases and then repeating those phrases to twenty or thirty strangers. Through repetition, you learn the phrases, and you make new friends. This method, however, is increasingly falling into disfavor. The LAMP method is useful for standard greetings and phrases, but it does not teach you how to be creative and develop sentences you've never before spoken. You speak only from a list of memorized phrases.

Newer methods suggest that you spend more time working with an individual language helper or assistant. This way, you receive personal input rather than just listening to speakers use large amounts of vocabulary you don't know. Then spend more time talking and interacting with a small circle of friends rather than parroting memorized phrases quickly to a large number of people.

Answer from Mike, who served ten years in West Africa and North Africa on a Bible translation team with WEC International.

A: Ask others to correct your language mistakes.

Ask people to correct your language, your pronunciation of words in the language they are teaching you. Don't be timid about asking, "Did I say it right?" They will readily correct your language— but only if you're willing and ask.

I remember hearing about an older woman who'd been a missionary for years in Africa. She consistently bungled the language those people had been trying to teach her, but she thought she was doing a wonderful job. One day a young African man had the boldness to correct that woman's language. She drew herself up to her full height and looked up at this tall Nuer man. She said, "Young man, I was speaking this language before you were born."

Don't follow that woman's example. Instead, ask people to correct your language, your manners, and your way of life, because there will be all kinds of new manners you're going to have to learn. Identify with people whenever possible in order to eliminate distractions. I am tall, white, blond, and blue-eyed. The Indians in the jungle of Ecuador are not tall, white, blond, or blue-eyed. There was no way I could change those things, but in every other possible way, I tried to identify with them. The first thing I did was to wear Indian dress, a simple navy blue skirt and a checked blouse.

Answer from Elisabeth Elliot, who worked with her husband Jim Elliot on translating the New Testament into the language of the Quichua Indians in Ecuador. Later, as a widow, she lived and worked among the Aucas.

DE-STRESSED CULTURE SHOCK

Language and geography may be the most obvious differences in living overseas. But a more obscure challenge is surviving culture shock and the continual stresses of living cross-culturally. Culture shock refers to the feelings of frustration, disorientation, and confusion experienced after relocating to a new environment.

Culture shock is very real, but missionaries in this section give some great ideas and insight for de-stressing culture shock.

Q: How do I learn to deal with culture shock?

A: Get good training before serving cross-culturally.

The key to handling culture shock is be thoroughly trained before going overseas. While there is no preventative cure, several things will help make you a more effective witness for Christ. For example, setting realistic expectations, focusing only on culture and language during the first year, bonding intentionally with nationals rather than hanging out with other expatriates, and resisting the temptation to communicate frequently with home.

Missionary Training International in Colorado Springs has excellent prefield training courses, if your agency does not provide this type of training (see "Resources for Further Study").

Answer from Jim, who has served with The Mission Society for ten years in Kazakhstan.

A: Train specifically for culture shock before you experience it.

Part of our mission's requirement for appointees is a month or more of prefield training that deals specifically with culture shock. We spent a month at the Center for Intercultural Studies in North Carolina, taking the equipping course and exploring topics such as transitions, worldview, ethnocentrism, culture theory, culture shock/culture stress, contextualization, cross-cultural communication, expectations, and more.

Understanding the culture is essential in dealing with culture shock. This is a process, but reading and observing will start you on your way. Another important factor is for you to understand that culture shock is a stress reaction that *will* happen—it's a predictable part of adjustment. Knowing your own vulnerabilities and struggles is also essential in adjusting to a culture. Know that your value is in Christ, not in what you do or in how you perceive that others feel about you. This is a healthy truth to savor, even in your home culture.

Read books on crossing cultures, such as *Ministering Cross-Culturally* by Lingenfelter and Mayers and *Cross-Cultural Connections* by Duane Elmer. Also, Marshall Cavendish Corporation publishes a series of books on different cultures called *CultureShock! A Survival Guide to Customs and Etiquette* (see "Resources for Further Study"). If you have a particular country in mind, this is a fantastic resource.

Answer from T. K., who has recently completed training to serve in Ireland with Greater Europe Mission.

THINGS NOBODY TOLD ME

If knowledge is power and honesty is a virtue, the missionaries in this section want to arm you with honest thoughts on the challenges they faced as new missionaries. A few of these real-life challenges include unrealistic expectations, spiritual warfare, boredom, and even the myth of superhuman missionaries.

Ponder, pray, seek counsel, and learn more about these "things nobody told me."

Q: What do missionaries wish they had known before they first worked cross-culturally?

A: I wish that I, and others, had realistic expectations of missionaries and of mission work.

Many people have unrealistic ideas of romantic bliss in marriage, without seeing the problems or day-to-day efforts needed to make a marriage work.

Missions is no different. In most missionary presentations, we hear only about the victories and great things the Lord is doing. I think that is for two reasons. First, missionaries are trying to recruit people into the work, so they strongly emphasize the positive side. Second, most people, and maybe especially missionaries, don't want to be vulnerable and reveal that they have problems. This is not helped by the fact that church people want to put missionaries on a superspiritual pedestal for being willing to sacrifice and live under harsh conditions. So it's important to talk with missionaries one-to-one to hear their struggles as well as their victories.

Another common fallacy is that the unsaved are crying out for someone to tell them the gospel. There may be the rare exception (in Papua New Guinea, one tribe did build a church in anticipation of the missionaries coming to tell them the good news), but in general, the unsaved are blinded. They are not searching for God and are living deceived in the darkness of their blinded condition. We will most commonly find indifference to the message, and at worst we'll experience downright opposition.

Missionaries who think they're going overseas to do a great work for Jesus amuse me. First, we merely participate in the work God is *already* doing. This is well explained in the book *Experiencing God* by Henry Blackaby (see "Resources for Further Study"). Of course, all our friends at home will tell us what a great and wonderful thing we're doing. Then WHAM! We come face-to-face overseas with all our inadequacies and weaknesses. We realize how much we're actually going to have to depend on God to see something accomplished. Many missionaries, confronted with the reality of living in a foreign culture and the time needed to influence people, simply become discouraged, turn around, and come home. Only when we realize our total dependence on God, wait on him, and work with him do we finally see some beautiful fruit.

Answer from Mike, who served ten years in West Africa and North Africa on a Bible translation team with WEC International.

A: I wish I had learned about spiritual warfare.

I wish I had known more about my relationship to God and about spiritual warfare. *Victory Over the Darkness* by Neil T. Anderson is one book every Christian should read (see "Resources for Further Study"). This book helps us understand and recognize spiritual warfare. Wherever we're living right now, we are in the middle of a battle. We need to understand the nature of that battle so that we can be victorious over our enemy. When we cross into another culture, where Satan has built strongholds for centuries and where cultural cues vary, the battle looks different. However, our victory over the powers of darkness is still in Christ.

Answer from Tim, who has served in Cameroon and in the United States with Wycliffe Bible Translators for twenty-five years.

Editor's Note: In addition to Neil T. Anderson's book, see also *Spiritual Warfare for Every Christian* by Dean Sherman (see "Resources for Further Study").

A: I wish I had known more about the physical and emotional challenges.

The following are some things nobody told me, but I'm telling you:

- *Boredom is real*. I heard that before I left my home country. But now I have long periods of downtime that I used to fill so easily at home. The first two months or so in a new place are the hardest, since you're establishing new friendships and a new pattern of life.
- *Knowing yourself is very important*. I have been stretched a phenomenal amount, especially in the first months of my assignment. If you have any hidden

personal issues, God will bring them to light. Be willing to deal with them as they come up; don't push them away. God needs to break you in order to use you.

- **Be teachable and be a lifelong learner**. It's easy to depend only on your ability to "figure it out once you get there," since firsthand knowledge may seem more dependable than book knowledge and theories. It's not true. Know before you go.
- **It takes time to ease into the structure**. At home, I had lots of energy to fill my day from early morning to late at night. But overseas I tire so quickly. Realize that being stretched physically, emotionally, and spiritually as well as facing a new culture, language, and living situation wears you out. It's OK to slow down. Being a missionary is not about being superhuman and accomplishing a long list each day. Some days all you'll accomplish is a trip to the grocery store or a government office. It's about trust, obedience, and hearing the Master's voice.

Answer from Bethany, who is serving in the Middle East with the Assemblies of God.

YES. NO. IT DEPENDS.

Did you notice in this chapter how often one response to a question disagreed with the previous response? Obviously, God prepares cross-cultural workers in different ways—because missionaries today serve in amazingly different ministries.

And, missionaries don't always serve in the same role. Often, their assignment changes, requiring additional training at different points throughout their lives. A turbo-quick illustration of how God might reassign you to one ministry focus after another is seen in the amazing to-do list of Philip in the Book of Acts.

Philip began his ministry as a waiter! Actually, he waited on tables as one of the apostles' seven deacons in the city of Jerusalem. His to-do list was to meet the needs of widows and orphans (Acts 6:1–6).

When severe persecution drove a majority of Christians out of Jerusalem, Philip launched into a new ministry as an evangelist in the neighboring near-culture of the Samaritans (see Acts 8:1–5). At the height of his work, Philip was suddenly commanded by God to journey far to the south—to the virtually deserted wilderness of Gaza. So Philip, beginning as a faithful deacon, became a powerful missionary evangelist.

Then God directed Philip into a pioneering-missionary role to reach an Ethiopian who was treasurer to the queen of the Ethiopians (Acts 8:26–40). Philip's ministry to the Ethiopian affected the spread of Christianity throughout most of northeastern Africa, even to this day.

And then? God miraculously translated Philip about twenty miles up the coast to the fishing village of Azotus. At that point, Philip must have sat with some hot, spiced coffee to consider the Roman-polished directional sign in the middle of town. He could take the road up through the hills back to his earlier ministry in Jerusalem. He could take another road east across the region to his rousing missionary-evangelist role in Samaria. Or he could head straight north toward his hometown of Caesarea.

It's as if God were giving Philip a captivating list of options for his next step in ministry. And God may lead you similarly into training for various ministry opportunities throughout your life.

MY THOUGHTS SO FAR

Some educational systems propagate the idea that if you simply study a subject for so many school years, you arrive at the level of a specialist. But as in almost every other field of work, the mission world acknowledges that education and training are actually lifelong processes.

Think back through this chapter's key questions. Then ask the Holy Spirit to guide you, through God's Word and through prayer, as you answer the questions below in light of what you *currently* understand from God. Finally, discuss your responses, concerns, and any unanswered questions with a leader or friend in your local church as you explore how you could become a missionary.

What are my current philosophies on mission training, both positive and negative? Which philosophies do I want to change?

_____

_____

_____

_____

What are my thoughts on foregoing a degree or training to go into missions now? What are the consequences of that decision, both positive and negative?

_____

_____

_____

_____

If I don't want advanced training, what role could I fill in missions as a "regular" Christian?

_____

_____

_____

_____

If I choose advanced training, what type(s) of training best fits God's guidance for me in cross-cultural missions?

_____

_____

_____

What training does the agency I'm interested in recommend?

_____

_____

_____

What mission-training options does my church offer?

_____

_____

_____

In what ways is God's guidance in my mission training still unclear?

_____

_____

_____

What might be the best way for me to learn a language?

_____

_____

_____

How can I prepare to deal with culture shock?

_____

_____

_____

In what ways can I train and prepare for cross-cultural missions today, right where I am?

_____

_____

_____

I will learn more about mission training in the following two ways (select from "Next Steps" and/or "Mission Courses," listed in "Resources for Further Study" at the end of this book):

1. _____

_____

_____

2. _____

_____

_____

FUNDING
Figuring It Out

5

THE COLD RAIN REFLECTED MY FRUSTRATION,
both spiritual and mechanical. Bill the mechanic mumbled, then
sang, *"S'a braw bricht moonlicht nicht the nicht"* in a Scottish brogue
as he examined my car. Finally, he sat to face me across the greasy
desk. "Quite a dent there on the door. And no doubt some motor
repair needed under the bonnet. Not used to driving on the left
side of the road, are you? But you say you're some sort of mission
worker?"

I mumbled a bit myself as I explained that I was *exploring* missions but not yet a bona fide missionary . . . and the finances of
that kind of ministry were still a concern . . . and no, I wasn't from
Scotland.

"Aye, now there's the shock," Bill laughed. "Listen, I'll fix
your car quick if you're interested in the missionary life—since
that's how I became a Christian."

After the general disinterest in religion I had seen in Scotland,
I leaned forward and asked, "So how did you come to faith in
Christ?" Then the mechanic with "Bill" sewn on his work shirt
taught me, the almost faithless missionary-to-be, a vivid lesson in
trusting God to provide for his kingdom workers.

"There was this missionary family—Steve and the wife and

little ones. He came in one day with a clunker; been given it by some friend who got more money off his new car without a trade-in. So the car got them from A to B for a bit, but then it blew a cylinder. So myself, I'm not a churchgoer, not a believer. I tell 'em there's no good news about their donated car. Yes, I could look for an engine, but I doubted I'd find one from a scrapped car. Finding a used engine that runs is like finding gold teeth on a chicken, but I said I'd call about and see if there was by any miracle an engine somewhere in the country. They walked out of the repair shop downcast. Somehow I felt concerned about these people, so during lunch break, I phoned about. A few minutes later I found a perfectly good engine for the vehicle right across town.

"So I called Steve and yelled in the phone, 'Pure-dead brilliant! I found one! We can collect it tomorrow morning. You need to pay two hundred pounds upfront, OK? It's a steal!'

"But Steve said the only money they had was two hundred pounds in the bank—and it's for taxes. They'd have to go when the bank opened at nine in the morning, get out all their money, and hope they could replace it before they had to pay their dues. He sounded like a depressed old lady when we hung up.

"Steve told me later that the two of 'em that night staggered off to bed, so low they could hardly pray. But the next morning the mail arrived especially early, at eight o'clock. There was this brown envelope with their names and address printed on the outside. The postmark said it had been mailed *two days before*. Steve said they opened it and both took a step back. No letter, just *two hundred pounds* in twenty notes! They had no idea where it came from. It had been in the post the past two days!"

Bill sat back at his greasy desk and laughed again. "So, that morning, in comes the whole family, right at half-past eight when I open the shop. 'You're lookin' bright and chirpy,' I told them—especially after our phone call last night.' Then Steve handed me a wad of twenty-pound notes. I know I started frowning, and I said, 'I'm thinking you had to go to the bank this morning to get the money . . . but, the bank's still shut now till nine.'

"Then they told me the money—*exactly what the engine cost*—was in the post that very morning. Steve showed me the envelope with the date of the mailing but with no name of who sent it. I sat down here on this desk, and something started clicking in my head.

"I knew these missionary people had been teaching a Bible club at my kids' school, and my kids came home every week and told me what they were learning in this club.

"So I asked Steve, 'You teach my children for free, don't you?' He just nodded.

"I said, 'Well, if your God has done this miracle with the engine money, then there must be something to it. I tell you what. I'll fix the engine for free, on one condition. You take me and my family to church.'"

Bill stood, slapped the clipboard on the desk, and said to me, "So we did just that. The car got a great engine. I got a brand new heart to follow Christ. And my family of new believers started going to church together."

I could only nod in amazement.

Then Bill, the wise Scottish mechanic, asked me, the faithless missionary-to-be, "You think that says anything to you this morning about money? About whether God can provide finances to serve in his kingdom work?"

Again I only nodded. My emergency car repair no longer seemed annoying. In a grease-smelling mechanic shop in cold, rainy Scotland, the Giver of all good things condescended to give my downcast heart the courage to believe that he *does* care for his own.

VALUABLE SUPPORT-RAISING ATTITUDES

Many mission-minded believers see fundraising as the number one obstacle to becoming a missionary. However, the support-raising phase of mission service is in itself a vital part of our ministry. Other Christians *want* to be closely involved in what God is doing in other cultures. So allowing them to supply part of our missionary income gives them a vital role.

Although funding may not be a popular discussion point in the typical mission presentation, it's definitely an important topic for aspiring missionaries and their families. Let's think through some of these finance-related questions so we can understand how God helps overcome fundraising obstacles in our journey into missions.

Q. What perspective should I take toward raising prayer and financial support?

A: Let God grow your faith.

Ultimately, it's God's responsibility to provide for us as we follow his leading. He is the Lord of the universe, for whom nothing is too difficult (Genesis 18:14). He even calls into existence things that do not yet exist (Romans 4:17). This is a source of great comfort. Sometimes, however, neither his calendar nor his pace are as rapid as we might wish. Abraham had to wait quite a while before he received the promise of his son Isaac. Remember, for God the issue is not simply money. He will use our support-raising experiences to develop other characteristics in us, such as faith, patience, and sensitivity to others.

In the following biblical passages, study God's faithful provisions to Abraham: Genesis 11:27–25:11; Romans 4; and Hebrews 11. Then consider Philippians 4:10–20, where Paul in every verse refers to his own experience in fundraising.

Raising support is actually a spiritual issue. Becoming a missionary means expecting God to enable us to communicate a message to people of another culture that will lead them to change their whole worldview. That is an unreal expectation from a human point of view. Only a miracle can accomplish this end. However, we believe in the God of miracles, who reached out to us and is changing us day by day, and we believe he can do this in others' lives as well. Similarly, if this God, who is the Creator and Sustainer of the universe, calls us to serve him, can he not also provide for our needs? As the mission we served under told us, "The provision of financial resources is God's seal on your direction to serve him in missions."

The great majority of American missionaries today have gone through the process of raising support. But it's not just garnering support. It is entering into a partnership with people who will commit themselves to share our vision, opportunities, trials, difficulties, and blessings. As Paul tells the Corinthians, "You also must help us by prayer, so that many will give thanks on our behalf for the blessing granted us through the prayers of many" (2 Corinthians 1:11, ESV).

Answer from Jack Voelkel, missionary-in-residence with the Urbana Student Mission Convention. Previously Jack served thirty years with Latin America Mission in Peru and Colombia.

A:  Resist the temptation to fear.

God did not give us a spirit of fear (2 Timothy 1:7). Think about it. If God is leading you, then who would like you to be so afraid of doing what it takes to become a missionary? The enemy! Resist the temptation to allow support raising to be a fearful experience or an obstacle that keeps you from going into missions.

Support raising simply means sharing with others the exciting vision God has given you. When people hear your heart (and God's direction) as you share, they *will* get involved. Usually support will come from sources you did not expect. Support raising is an exciting faith-walk with God.

As you meet with people to share your mission vision, *listen* to the leading of the Holy Spirit. This takes some practice, and you may make some mistakes at first. For example, when you meet with a pastor, a missions committee, or an individual, know that the Holy Spirit will guide you in what to say and do. And follow the peace of Christ in the decisions that you make. If you don't have peace, move on and don't dwell on it. When you sense the peace of the Lord, you can be confident that God is at work, making a divine connection to your support team.

Answer from Kelly, a missionary in Southeast Asia.

A: Avoid sales pressure as well as presumption.

My experience over the last decade as a faith-supported missionary is that I've had lots of fears and confusion regarding financial support. But it all boils down to two questions. When I answer yes to both of them, everything is OK. When I don't answer yes, I consistently run into problems. Here are the questions:

1. Do I trust that God will take care of me and not "hang me out to dry"?
2. Am I asking God for provision each day ("Give us this day our daily bread") and accepting each day's provision with heartfelt thankfulness?

Some type of formal training in raising support is a good idea. Scriptural teaching on support raising is crucial, as is learning from the experiences of others. Training is important, since missionaries all too easily fall to one extreme or the other—humanistic sales strategies or presumptuous faith.

Answer from Nate Wilson, a mission mobilizer with Caleb Project.

A: Never doubt God's involvement and provision.

When I was preparing to serve short-term, I estimated the amount of money I needed per month to stay for eight months. As I put money into my savings account, I thought I had enough money for this short-term trip. So when people asked me about the finances I would need, I told them that my savings would cover the trip.

Just before leaving, however, I had several unexpected expenses, including new eyeglasses. Then, when I arrived in Equatorial Guinea, my expenses were higher than I had expected, and I quickly realized I had enough funds to last only about four months. I also realized that I needed to extend my time in Equatorial Guinea for an additional seven months to accomplish the work I was there to do.

What did I do? I began to pray about the situation. God answered in a marvelous way. He led a few friends to send support—even though they were unaware that I needed it. I finished the fifteen months and never lacked in finances. Praise to his name!

Answer from Mike, who served ten years in West Africa and North Africa on a Bible translation team with WEC International.

A: Let courage and truth guide you.

You who will face the rigors of field living must have a strong, God-given assurance that this is his will for you. It's critical to follow the guidance of Colossians 3—to let the Word of God dwell richly in your heart, to let the peace of Christ rule decisively in all issues, and, in whatever you do, to do it as unto the Lord.

Your conviction must be as strong as David's, when he faced the stoning of his men as they returned to Ziklag: "But David strengthened himself in the LORD his God" (1 Samuel 30:6 ESV). Further, your heart must have the confidence of Philippians 1:6: "He who began a good work in you will carry it on to completion."

Remind and encourage yourself in the following truths:

- People are not giving money to you. As you give your life to the work of the Lord, people give their finances *to him*.
- It's a privilege to be about the Father's business (read the story of Esther).
- Live a lifestyle as close as possible to those among whom you will minister, even as Jesus did: "The Word became flesh and made his dwelling among us" (John 1:14). Jesus didn't stay in five-star hotels! He also said, "As the Father has sent me, I am sending you" (John 20:21). Read Philippians 2 to understand *how* he was sent.
- Commit 100 percent of your personal resources to God. "It's all yours, Lord!" Be a faithful steward of what has been entrusted to you.

- God owns all, yet he is the most frugal economist. He wastes nothing. It's not a matter of "tightening your belt"! It's a matter of strategically spending your resources.

Answer from Neal Pirolo, missionary trainer and author of I Think God Wants Me to Be a Missionary *(see "Resources for Further Study").*

A: Learn now to discuss difficult things.

Raising support is difficult for most people. Your mission agency will have information, advice, and perhaps even training in this area. Talking to your pastor and church missions committee may also help you develop a more positive attitude for support raising.

For many aspiring missionaries, if they don't have the support, they don't go to the mission field. If you keep that in mind, then raising support is just another step toward the place you believe the Lord wants you.

Talking about needs and asking for support is a difficult thing. But then, speaking about Christ to the lost can be just as difficult. Support raising is one way to help you develop an ability to talk about something difficult with people who may or may not be positive in their response.

Answer from John in Japan, where he has been a missionary for five years.

BEGGING OR BEING SENT?

Sometimes aspiring missionaries are nervous about the funding necessary for missions service. Although some missionaries accepted by a denominational agency are guaranteed a salary, nearly 80 percent of missionaries are sent from faith-based agencies and have raised their own support.

While the financial aspects of service seem intimidating, be encouraged by Jesus' own fundraising miracle in Matthew 17:27. Jesus had a pressing need, a real need, a monetary need. Knowing that his Father would provide, Jesus said to Peter, "Go to the lake and throw out your line. Take the first fish you catch; open its mouth and you will find a four-drachma coin. Take it and give it to them for my tax and yours." As Jesus lived each day, fulfilling God's mission, God always provided, sometimes turning water into wine, sometimes multiplying fish and bread, and sometimes catching fish until the boat sank. God does and will provide for his own—always.

Like many, however, you may still feel that raising support is asking for personal charity. Here are some answers from missionaries who had those same feelings before they began their journey.

Q. If I feel raising support is begging, is there any other way to raise support?

A: I too thought it was begging—at first.

At first, I also hated the idea of raising support and viewed it as begging for money. But now I'm so glad for the experience. It forced me to clearly share my vision. It forced me to talk to people I didn't know. It forced me to deal with people, even pastors, who questioned different aspects of who I am and what I would do, such as differences in doctrinal emphases, mission strategies, and church priorities. Now when I see listed each month the dozens of people who give to my support (and dozens more who don't give financially but who pray), I am confident that God has put me where he wants me. Many of the people who support me through finances and prayer were strangers to me before I began raising support. Now they are vital partners in what I'm doing in youth evangelism in Japan.

Answer from John, who has served in Japan for nine years with SEND International.

A: Read what the Bible says about financial partners.

Many people are supported after going from person to person and from church to church because it is a biblical model. You are not begging. Children of Jehovah Jireh *never* have to beg.

A missionary is in every sense also a mission mobilizer, and you will be mobilizing partners for God's vision. This means that you give *them* an opportunity to go and work in a far-off country. If they cannot go, then you also give them the offer for you to do it in their stead. You do the work for them, you keep them informed, and you pray for them. On the other hand, they pay for your joint ministry, they pray for you and your joint ministry, and they help you recruit for your joint ministry. The word *support* should be replaced in our vocabulary and in our attitudes with the word *partner*.

Answer from Paul, who is serving in South Africa with Operation Mobilization.

A: Humbly depend only on the Provider.

Among the opportunities opened to us through support raising, the first is the opportunity to gain humility. It sure looks like begging before you begin, especially if you're coming from the business world as I did. But as you consider God, his purposes, and his church, the scenario changes. I no longer see it as begging. God, who is sending me, will provide for me—through his church. It's just a matter of being led to the people whom God has already chosen to give support. If you want success, begin your service in humility.

The second great opportunity opened to us through support raising is the opportunity to depend fully on the Provider rather than depending on our own capacities, knowledge, abilities, and relationships.

Third is the opportunity to see specific prayers clearly answered. For example, I prayed that my supporters would come from this area, which would limit my traveling during furloughs. God graciously granted both.

Answer from Moisés, a Mexican mobilizing Mexican individuals and Spanish-speaking churches. He has served with OC International and the U.S. Center for World Mission.

A: Adjust your attitude.

The framing of this question (Is there any way other than begging to raise support?) causes me to wonder if those asking are certain that God desires them in missions. If they are called, then sharing the ministry is part of involving other believers in kingdom advancement. "Going from church to church" is not about begging for money. It's relating how you are answering God's invitation to proclaim Christ to those who need to hear. Making known the need for financial support allows others to participate in and affirm your future work, and you gain a deeper trust in God (you'll need that deeper trust, I'm sure).

If faith missions is still too uncomfortable, consider either your denomination's mission board, which may subsidize missionaries, or tentmaking, in which you may receive a stipend or salary. But first, ask God what he intends for you, both in your overseas work and how to fund it.

Answer from Karen, who served with HCJB World Radio in Ecuador for eleven years.

A: Invite others to join God in what he is doing.

If you're afraid of support raising, get over it! Unless you are independently wealthy, you'll have to do it.

As for how to get over any specific fear, you probably already know the right things to do: pray, talk to folks who have already overcome their fear of support raising, study relevant Scripture, read all the books on support raising you can find, and then jump in and begin.

Fundraising is still my least favorite part, and the hardest part, of being a missionary, but I no longer dread it as I once did. I have changed my attitude from "I'm asking for money" to "I'm telling people about what God is doing (or wants to do) and giving them a chance to be part of it."

Answer from Jay, an independent missionary who has been working in Italy for five years.

A: Consider tentmaking or business-as-mission.

Some jobs allow you to earn your living while you serve. In missions, this is sometimes called "tentmaking," since the apostle Paul earned a salary as a tentmaker during his missionary journeys. But beware: earning your living will likely consume way more of your time than you realize. To learn more about tentmaking, connect with the organization Global Opportunities (GlobalOpps.org).

One of the most important components of fundraising for

missions is getting people to pray for you. If you're not asking your friends and family for prayer, don't even think about going into missions.

Answer from Jack Voelkel.

A: Don't allow fear or pride to limit God.

One approach is to be a tentmaker. In many needy fields, any number of tentmaking skills could be applied to earning an adequate income at the local standard of living (not necessarily at your home standard of living, however).

A real option is to humble yourself and do what is required to obey God, even if it's something you don't want to do. I hated the thought of traveling around to ask people for money. But I knew God was leading that way, so I faced the situation and did it. God blesses obedience and humility. He has a hard time working with pride and with those of us who set limits on what we will or won't do for him.

Answer from Jay, who served in Italy eleven years, the first three years as a tentmaker.

A: To preach to those who haven't heard of Jesus, we must first be sent.

My answer to this question comes from Romans 10:14–15:

> How, then, can they call on the one they have not believed in? And how can they believe in the one of whom they have not heard? And how can they hear without someone preaching to them? And how can they preach unless they are sent? As it is written, "How beautiful are the feet of those who bring good news!"

We see three groups of people here: the unsaved, the senders, and the goers. The missionary, as the goer, communicates between the other two groups. Because we must be sent, raising the support of senders is part of our job.

Answer from Dale Pugh, who is international coordinator for World International Mission and served long term in Mexico.

EFFECTIVE SUPPORT-RAISING APPROACHES

Perhaps the possibility of raising support still seems overwhelming. In any case, let's investigate various ways missionaries raise financial and prayer support. As you read the following approaches (the Bible has a variety of examples), God will counsel and encourage you in ways to raise support—with him as your provider.

Q: What can I do to successfully raise prayer and financial support?

A: Combine faith-filled prayer with fearless communication.

I believe that where God guides, he provides. Yet, just as I learned how to preach, I also had to learn to raise support. The way

I have raised support is by fearlessly praying and communicating.

First, I pray to find out what God wants me to do, and then through prayer I apply his promises to those needs. Second, in an honest and up-front way, I share with my home church and prayer partners what I intend to do and what I need to get the job done. I have never begged for money. Instead, after praying about my needs, church leaders and supporters usually ask what I need. Sometimes the Lord gives me creative ways to share those needs in a newsletter or through some other communication with my support team.

Answer from Dale Pugh, who is international coordinator for World International Mission and served long term in Mexico.

A. Give generously to missionaries now and receive from others later.

Over twenty years ago, I quit my job as a pharmacist to join Campus Crusade for Christ. I needed to raise a significant amount of support per month plus some for one-time needs. One thing I recall is that I had given generously to different mission organizations in the previous years, above the tithe to my church. As I gave, Luke 6:38 applied: "Give, and it will be given to you."

I somewhat naively thought that the Lord could bring these pledges together in about thirty days. Praise God, he did exactly that. And my home church pledged nothing that first year.

Answer from Tom in Slovakia, where he has been a missionary for seven years.

A. Follow the example of George Müller—trust God alone.

WEC's tradition of trusting God alone for provision comes from scriptural examples and the influence of the life of George Müller. In the 1800s, Müller was guided by God to begin an orphanage in

Bristol, England, by faith in the promises of God. He made no appeal for funds, but rather sought God to move in people's hearts so they would give toward the care of the orphans. Müller's testimony to God's faithful provision influenced Hudson Taylor, founder of the China Inland Mission, and later C. T. Studd, founder of WEC, who began his mission career with Taylor in China.

Reflect on the words of George Müller:

> Over the years the Lord has faithfully taken care of us financially in our work of caring for the orphans by constantly raising up new supporters. God's promise is that they that trust in the Lord shall never be confounded . . . for one reason or another were we to lean upon man we would inevitably be disappointed; but, in leaning upon the living God alone, moment by moment, we are beyond disappointment and beyond being forsaken because of death, or of not having enough to live on or enough love or because of the needs of other works also requiring support. How precious to have learned to stand with God alone in the world, and yet to be happy and confident, and to know that "no good thing will He withhold from them that walk uprightly."[1]

Some who read or hear of Müller's adventures of faith say, "Oh, he had a special gift of faith, but I couldn't live like that!" Müller argues, "It is the selfsame faith which is found in every believer . . . Oh, I plead with you, do not think me an extraordinary believer, having privileges above others of God's dear children, which they cannot have, nor look on my way of acting as something that would not do for other believers. Do but stand still in the hour of trial, and you will see the help of God if you trust in Him."[2]

Answer from Jim Raymo, former U.S. director of WEC International. Jim has been a missionary in Europe, Asia, and at WEC USA headquarters.

HOW MUCH IS ENOUGH?

Q: How much money should a missionary raise, and how long should it take?

A: The cost of living varies widely from country to country.

Costs vary according to the country, situation, family size, and mission agency's requirements. A single missionary in some countries can get by on the equivalent of US$500 a month—without transportation and children's school fees. A married couple with five children in a mission school and a 4-wheel-drive vehicle could need well above US$5,000 a month.

Answer from Bill, serving with Into All The World. He served for thirty-two years in Africa and Asia.

A: The money needed depends on where you serve; the time needed to raise it depends on your effort.

The biggest factors in knowing *how much* money you have to raise are where you will be serving and whether you will live in individual or team housing. For example, serving in rural areas of countries in the two-thirds world normally means you need less support than serving in western Europe.

Support raising is based on relationships, so the *timing* is based on how much time you invest in building relationships beforehand as well as how many appointments you make to speak to people about support raising. My wife and I met with ninety-six family units over four months before we were 100 percent supported. I know others who have raised full support in ninety days. On the other hand, another person in one year raised only 65 percent.

Either you or the agency can set a deadline, but both of you should agree to it.

Answer from Rob, who has served for six years with Operation Mobilization.

A: Set a deadline.

You should have a deadline, because deadlines create urgency. And urgency motivates not only the donor to give and pray on your behalf, but it also motivates you to be proactive in your search for funds and to be dependent upon the Lord, who has called you to accomplish his purposes.

Urgency calls for decisions. When you ask for critically needed funds with established deadlines, prospective or existing donors move from "Maybe we will think about helping you sometime" mode into "We need to make a decision now" mode, "so we can help our brother or sister in Christ who has been guided by the Lord to accomplish this particular vision."

Deadlines can be powerfully effective, and I've watched some amazing things take place as people and ministries set deadlines. Maybe you need to review the vision the Lord has given you and keep in mind that it's really not your vision but the Lord's agenda you need to accomplish.

Answer from Bill Dillon, author of People Raising *(see "Resources for Further Study").*

Q: Can I go overseas before I have all my funds raised?

A: No. Aim for 110 percent.

It's better for you to shoot for raising 110 percent of your support and to have those funds committed before you leave for the mission field. Most missionaries lose 5–15 percent of their support during the first two years of service, so leaving home before you are at least fully funded is a recipe for financial disaster.

God has all the money you need to serve in missions, but sadly it's in other people's wallets—and many of them forgot to have their wallets baptized.

Answer from Rob, who has served ten years with Operation Mobilization.

A: No. Going without full support is not wise.

Maintaining funds on the field can be difficult enough, but trying to raise additional funds while on the field is even harder. One of my colleagues went to the field after raising 80 percent of her support because she felt she was under a time crunch to get there. But suddenly, she barely had enough money for food. In addition, the currency exchange rate was suffering, so she was forced to go back home to raise more support. I highly suggest not only being fully supported before you go but also having some funds built up in your account to cover losses from supporters who either are late on gifts or end their support.

Answer from J. B., who serves in the former Soviet Union.

A: Yes. Trust God for all your financial needs.

My husband and I have been with a faith mission for thirty-two years. We have never been without all that we need. Has our support always been 100 percent? Perhaps not for what we *wanted*, but always for what we *needed*.

Many mission agencies allow you to go to your assigned country with 80 percent of your financial support raised. You may think, *I just can't go unless I have raised 100 percent of my support; otherwise, how will I make ends meet?* If that's your concern, then you may trust more in money than in God, who promised to provide all you need.

Some see their support jump to 100 percent after they leave their home country. God wants to know if we are willing to obey him and trust him to provide. The time is short, and so many people need to hear the good news. Don't limit God. Do your part: share the ministry and stay in contact with all the people God leads you to write or call. Then leave the rest to him.

Don't allow the pressures of fundraising to build so that you're begging God to let you go to your assigned country. Pray and move ahead. God *will* provide all you need, either by moving in the hearts of his people to support you, or he will provide in other practical ways.

Answer from Carol, who has served with TEAM for thirty-two years in Sri Lanka, India, and the Persian Gulf.

PAID OFF AND DEBT FREE

Another obstacle that many prospective missionaries face is financial debt. If you are in training now, here are solutions for minimizing school debt. If you already owe money, read on to learn ways to deal with debt on your journey into missions.

Q: How can I minimize financial debt while in training?

A: Borrow as little as possible.

Scripture does not prohibit borrowing money, but it is discouraged. "The borrower is servant to the lender" (Proverbs 22:7). Christians should not be slaves to anyone. A healthy goal for all Christians is to live debt free so they can serve the Lord and give their tithes and offerings with joy and abandon. Therefore, borrowing should be entered into with great caution, with a plan to borrow as little as possible and to repay as soon as possible.

Money should be borrowed for needs only, not for wants. The best way to differentiate between needs and wants is to live on a budget and to buy only budgeted items. Christians borrowing money, especially those of us going into missions, should live a missionary lifestyle from the beginning. We should realize that our significance is derived from who we are in Christ, not from what we own or whether we have the trendiest clothing and the most sought-after designer labels.

Comb through the lists of available scholarships in the financial-aid office and apply for many. Avoid unsubsidized educational loans unless there is no possible alternative. At the end of each year, the accumulated interest is capitalized, and this plunges us deeper into debt.

Seek counsel on financial management from godly counselors.

Answer from David Topazian, DDS, executive director of MedSend. David served with TEAM in South America for six years.

A: Work part-time and study part-time.

I'm in favor of prefield missionary training, but I am not in favor of incurring large debt from that training. One practical consideration is to study part-time and be gainfully employed at the same time to pay the school bill as it occurs, which gives us time to assimilate, apply, and practice the information and training we receive before going abroad. This should not be a frustrating process. After all, if training is God's will for the missionary candidate, then developing character through fiscal responsibility and responsible debt payment is also a part of his training program.

Answer from Ron Meyers, who served as a missionary in Korea for thirteen years and in China for five years.

A: Receive financial support during your education.

I believe that, to the extent possible, every church in America should support at least one seminary or Bible college student with exactly the same commitment they do a missionary or any other ministry. I also happen to believe that more families should pray about becoming personally involved in helping to train somebody to minister in areas where they cannot go themselves.

Most ministries, and some missionaries, have the ability to let their needs be known. But in reality, average seminary students have a very difficult time, or even fear, speaking out about their own needs. Christians shouldn't be beggars, but on the other hand, God's Word does not prohibit asking or letting a need be known—as best I can tell. If all Christians were totally attuned to the Holy Spirit and could sense every need of God's people, these students would never have to ask for help. God depends on those who are attuned to support those who have needs.[3]

Answer from Larry Burkett, founder of Christian Financial Concepts.

Q: How do I handle my debts and still go into missions?

A: Follow a loan repayment plan or include loan payments in your mission budget.

Debt in my opinion is one of the biggest hindrances for college graduates and for families wanting to serve in missions. The choices we make in this area can affect whether we get to the field. I recently read that the average college student graduates over thirty-thousand dollars in debt. Two approaches to handling debt are to pay off the debt before leaving for the field or to include loan payments in your mission budget and go now.

If the first plan is best for you (it was for me), a *loan amortization* computer program can calculate a specific schedule for paying off the loans. This plan can include how much to pay and for how long. Stick to that plan as if your life depends on it. The people I knew from college who had no loan repayment plan never made it overseas. Without a plan, they lost focus when the debt wasn't easily paid off.

So make a budget that first deducts your tithe, housing, and food, and then pay more than your plan calls for each month. Pray for supernatural bonuses and raises, and when they come, apply the extra to paying off debt. Finally, stay involved in short-term missions so that you don't forget what God has led you to do.

If the second plan is best for you, start packing your bags and get moving toward raising support. Don't be ashamed to add a certain amount of money into your budget to repay student loans, and don't hide behind a rock when people ask about it.

For most students coming out of college, I recommend this second plan. Here's why. In my experience, many mission-minded people are not able to land jobs that pay enough to kill debt fast (because their degrees are not in demand). While the ideal is a high-paying job, many end up working in a position that pays barely enough to live on. Lest you feel guilty for asking others to pay your school debt, never forget that God wants you to go!

No matter which plan you follow, trust God to take care of it. You never know what will happen as you move in faith into missions.

Answer from Kyle, a missionary with Pioneers, serving with his wife and two children in Asia.

A: Obey God's guidance, and he will provide.

You must follow the leadership of the Holy Spirit in all that you do. When we left our secular careers for Bible school, we had a lot of personal debt, but God always met our needs. When we left for the mission field, we had some personal debt again. As we prayed about this, we sensed God's peace, and while we were on the field we were able to pay off our debts.

I think the key issue is being sensitive to God's will for each of us. When we are faithful to do our best to obey, God will provide for our needs.

We learned an important principle: when in doubt, DON'T! If you don't sense the clear guidance of God in a decision you're making, the best advice is not to act until you know in your spirit what God desires you to do. Don't get impatient and react on emotion or logic, but rather trust and wait on the Lord.

Answer from Kelly, serving in Southeast Asia.

A: Work hard, live frugally, and pay the debt.

I would say work hard for a couple of years, live very frugally, and pay off your debts. Find ways to decrease your expenses and pay down debt as fast as you can. While God has the ability to provide everything immediately, he may well have practical and academic lessons for you to learn.

Some mission agencies, including WEC, are making provision for student loans. If missionary candidates present to WEC a letter from a supporter (person or church) promising to pay down the school loans for as long as the missionaries are with WEC, then we ignore the debt. This provision applies only to school loans.

Credit-card debt must be paid off before applicants can become candidates. If they have a home mortgage and want to keep the house, they must find someone to act as their property manager, renting the house at a rate that covers the mortgage, taxes, and other related fees.

Finally, and I saved the best for last, pray. Some who have joined our mission have received gifts of thousands of dollars to apply toward indebtedness. This has been such a blessing for missionary candidates, raising their trust level several points.

Answer from David Smith, director of mobilization with WEC International. David has been a missionary for twenty-five years as a field worker in West Africa and at WEC USA headquarters.

A: Ask God to help you get out of debt before you go.

We had strong convictions to be out of debt before we went on the mission field. Once we arrived, we were so glad to be out of debt. The families under the most stress and anxiety were the ones who had left debts behind at home. While this may have been just our experience, it was sad to see what some families were going through. Their budgets were tight, much of our fellowship time together was spent on their finances, and they were not free to minister as they wanted. Two families had to return home to take care of the bills. Pray that God will quickly provide the finances for you to clear your debts.

When we decided to go overseas, we owed a mortgage on a house in a section of town where property was devaluing faster than anyone could have expected. We put our house on the market and began praying. Our house sold in one month. We made two thousand dollars on the house. That may not seem much, but the house next to ours took two years to sell, and the owners lost ten thousand dollars on the sale. Our houses were identical. God does take care of us. During the three years we were overseas, we never lacked for funds. While we did not have an abundance, God took care of our every need. He also gave us some of our wants.

Answer from Karin, who served as an English teacher in China for five years.

A: Look into MedSend grants if you will be a medical missionary.

If you are headed to a career in medical missions, learn about Project MedSend. These educational-loan repayment grants are for qualified applicants who have borrowed carefully, lived a restrained lifestyle, and started repaying at the first opportunity. Project MedSend provides financial counsel and resources that help health professionals in training or prehealth students learn more about Christian financial management.

Answer from David Topazian, DDS, executive director of MedSend. David served with TEAM in South America for six years.

READY TO RETIRE

While the question of debt deals with the past, the issue of retirement looks to the future. Proverbs 30:25 states, "Ants are creatures of little strength, yet they store up their food in the summer." Following the wisdom of Solomon, missionaries share in this section different ways to prepare for retirement.

Q: In what ways do missionaries plan for retirement?

A: Some agencies assist with retirement packages.

Some supporting churches want to require agencies to provide their missionaries a decent retirement and medical-care package, although some of the same churches occasionally complain about the total cost. It's a bit difficult, however, for retirement plans to be both responsible and inexpensive.

Our mission, WEC, is one of the agencies that allows missionaries a variety of retirement packages, ranging from nothing at all to whatever they can afford on their support.

Some are concerned that if we allow missionaries to serve with little or no financial provision for the future, they may not have a future. History is on our side. We began as a mission in 1913, and we presently have two thousand missionaries. WEC has had a multitude of missionaries retire in the years of our existence—and no retiree has ever been destitute, because God has always provided. Some have gone to retirement centers in Florida built specifically for missionaries from faith agencies. Some have had houses given to them. Some have gone to live with siblings or children. We even have retirement units at our WEC campus.

Answer from David Smith, director of mobilization with WEC International. David has been a missionary for twenty-five years as a field worker in West Africa and at WEC USA headquarters.

A: Start early contributing each month to a retirement fund.

I believe that you, the missionary, should plan to provide most of your retirement income needs yourself. Why? (1) Many agencies barely assist with retirement planning. (2) Most have retirement programs that go with you after you leave the agency, but some do not. (3) You may be totally committed to the vision of your agency and can't imagine leaving it. But if the senior leadership changes and a new vision is adopted, or if God calls you in a different direction, you are solely responsible for your retirement.

I'm a missionary sent by a local church that has no retirement plan. So I'm preparing for my retirement by including in my budget a monthly contribution to a retirement fund. For a small fee, a good accountant or financial planner can give you specific retirement advice. Or at no cost you can research retirement planning for yourself.

The most important retirement savings advice is to start early. Those who wait until later to begin saving have to save a higher portion of their income than those who begin earlier.

Answer from Jay, an independent missionary who served in Italy for ten years.

A: Store up treasures in heaven while God provides on earth.

I subscribe to Jesus' plan from Matthew 6:20: "Store up for yourselves treasures in heaven." I left for the mission field with three thousand dollars in my pocket and all my possessions sold. A church of only twenty-five members had sent me, but they had not promised to support me financially. I arrived in North Africa, and two weeks later my money had grown tenfold. I lived the next three years on this amount.

Yes, I was imprisoned, terrorized, robbed, had my life threatened dozens of times, and was thrown out of two countries. My retirement fund is looking good in heaven with Jesus where it belongs. Here on earth my treasure is not. My years in missions were truly a joyful experience that I would not trade for an IRA or a 401K.

Answer from Jack, who served in North Africa for five years.

A: Trust God to provide at retirement age.

John Wesley said, "Earn all you can, save all you can, give all you can!" As missionaries, we can't "earn all you can," but we can save and give. "Give, and it will be given to you" is a promise you can bet your retirement on (Luke 6:38).

Answer from Tom, who has served for nineteen years in Philippines and Slovakia with Campus Crusade for Christ.

VISION. SACRIFICE. PERSEVERANCE.

Ten miles south of Ensenada in Baja California, Highway 1 meanders through the slums of Maneadero, Mexico. It's there that Pastor Lorenzo has modeled for us all how to expect God's provision for ministry.

With no initial funding, he convinced an architect to draw plans for his dream of a new church building. The vision of a beautiful church in a rough slum was stunning.

The Mexican pastor began digging the foundation with his own shovel, and soon his impoverished church members joined him. Visitors, touring through the town on their way to south-Baja holidays, noticed the work, caught the vision, and joined in the effort.

Over a challenging three years, the pastor, his entire congregation, tourists from California, churches from other regions, and three expert bricklayers erected a beautiful center of worship.

The fulfillment of this dream offers all aspiring missionaries the principles by which our ministries can be funded:

Vision attracts resources.

Sacrifice inspires others to participate.

Perseverance gives God time to work on our behalf.

This simple reminder of God's provision compels us—as does the psalmist's repetition of the Hebrew term *selah*—to "pause and meditate."

MY THOUGHTS SO FAR

As you trust that God *will* provide for his ministry, think back through this chapter's key questions. Then ask the Holy Spirit to guide you, through God's Word and through prayer, as you answer the questions below in light of what you *currently* understand from God. Finally, discuss your responses, concerns, and any unanswered questions with a leader or friend in your local church as you explore how you could become a missionary.

What are my perspectives, both positive and negative, toward raising prayer and financial support?

_____

_____

_____

_____

How can I correct my negative perspectives and attitudes?

_____

_____

_____

_____

How is raising financial support as a missionary different from begging for personal charity?

_____

_____

_____

Has God ever allowed uncomfortable circumstances in my life—for my personal growth? What was the outcome? Could raising support be a similarly uncomfortable step God has planned for me?

_____

_____

_____

_____

_____

With what approaches could I successfully raise prayer and financial support?

_____

_____

_____

How can I minimize or eliminate my financial debts?

_____

_____

_____

_____

From Philippians 4:10–20, what can I learn from the apostle Paul's own fundraising in his work as a missionary?

_____

_____

_____

_____

I will learn more about mission funding in the following two ways (select from the books and courses listed in "Resources for Further Study" at the end of this book):

1. _____

_____

2. _____

_____

SINGLES, COUPLES, AND KIDS
Counting the Cost

6

SHE STOOD IN THE MILDEWED HALLWAY ON THE tenth floor of the tenement. The late-afternoon Swedish sun was softening as she knocked on a dirty steel door.

"Vem er han den?" an old man muttered through the door.

"It's Aina. Aina Flood, Daddy," she answered.

Hearing no response, she teared up. "It's your daughter, Papa. Aina. *Behaga öppen dörren.*"

He yanked the door open until the chain snagged. The stench of alcohol oozed through the gap.

"Aina? No!" His stubbled face crinkled as he squinted into the light. "Aina? I left Aina in the Congo a lifetime ago."

"My mama was your Svea. Open the door, Daddy."

That name, Svea, opened the door—and the old man's eyes, dulled by cataracts.

Aina, a grown woman now called Aggie Hurst, entered the dark apartment and David Flood's smelly life. He stumbled to a cot and choked out, "I never intended to give you away. I am so, so sorry."

Aggie knelt beside the bed. "It's all right, Papa." Tenderly she held his bony arm and said, "God took care of me."

David Flood shouted, "God? God forgot all of us. Our lives

have been ruined because of him." And David turned his face to the wall.

Into the darkening room Aggie declared, "Papa, you *did not* go to Africa in vain. Mama *did not* die in vain."

More than three decades earlier, David Flood was a shining new missionary sent from the Philadelphia Church in Stockholm. He and his twenty-seven-year-old bride Svea launched into the heart of what was then the Belgian Congo. Carrying their two-year-old son, the Floods and a couple named Erikson had slashed with machetes through nearly a hundred miles of jungle to the remote village of N'dolera.

But the enraged village elders drove them out of N'dolera for blaspheming the tribal gods. Undefeated, the two families climbed a nearby slope, built mud huts, and prayed for God to break through.

Breakthrough never came.

Twice a week, five-year-old Ruhigita Ndagora from the village took eggs and chickens to sell to the missionaries. Svea, working on her tribal language skills, told and retold the boy about the death, burial, and resurrection of Jesus Christ.

Months of primitive living and hostility from the locals finally pressed the Eriksons to leave the village and return to the Congo's central settlement. But the Floods would not leave. Svea became pregnant, but eight months later, weakened by malaria, her health broke. Seventeen days after giving birth to Aina in the little mud hut, Svea died.

David Flood, weeping over his wife's lifeless body in his arms, staggered out and buried Svea in a crude grave. Then he stopped a young N'dolera man on a trail and convinced him to carry the seventeen-day-old girl for him. Flood strapped his older child onto his back, and they trekked the hundred miles back to civilization.

He found the Eriksons, placed the starving baby Aina on a table, and snarled, "I'm returning to Sweden. I have lost my wife, and I cannot take care of this baby. *God* has ruined my life."

Nine months later, the Eriksons, both dying from being poisoned by hostile locals, handed Aina off to American missionaries Arthur and Anna Berg, who changed Aina's name to Aggie.

Three years later, the Bergs returned to the United States to launch a ministry among Native Americans. More than a decade after moving to America, Aggie enrolled in Bible college, where she met and then married Dewey Hurst, who was eventually appointed president of Northwest Bible College near Seattle.

One foggy Washington morning, Aggie Hurst led her two toddlers across the lawn to check the mailbox. Among the envelopes Aggie found a worn Christian magazine written in Swedish. With no idea who had sent it, Aggie thumbed through the pages until an article's photo stopped her cold. The photo was of a grave in a jungle bearing a white cross. Inscribed on the cross was a faded name, Svea Flood.

Aggie grabbed the kids and rushed to a translator at the college, who summarized the article for her. In the village of N'dolera, a boy had found salvation in Jesus Christ. As a young man, he persuaded the chief elders of the village to allow him to build a school. Soon all the students, their parents, and then the tribal chief became followers of Christ . . . all because of the sacrifice of David and Svea Flood.

And so Aggie Hurst, now sitting in the squalid tenement flat in Sweden, unfolded to her father the events that followed her finding the Swedish magazine in her Seattle mailbox.

"Papa. The college gave us a twenty-fifth anniversary gift to come here, to Sweden. So two days ago, in a stopover in London . . . Papa, we found Ruhigita Ndagora—the boy who brought you eggs and chickens in the jungle.

During that stopover, Aggie and her husband had strolled across the gardens of Royal Prince Albert Hall. Peeking inside the hall, they realized that an African man was about to speak to a mission convention. He was introduced as the leader of a movement of 110,000 believers and as one who had established thirty-two mission bases, several Bible schools, and a Christian hospital. Following the man's presentation, Aggie pressed forward to ask the speaker if he had ever heard of her birth parents, David and Svea Flood.

The speaker, visibly shaken by Aggie's question, secured a translator to cry out, *"Oui,* madame. Svea Flood led me to Jesus! I am the boy who brought food to your mama and papa before you were born. Your mother's grave and her memory are honored by everyone in the village. They have all come to faith in Christ."

"And then, Daddy," Aggie said as she stroked her father's fevered head, "Ruhigita opened his arms to hug me. He said we must come to Africa to see that David and Svea Flood are the most famous people in their village's history."

Aggie, her husband, and David Flood spent the rest of the daylight talking—old David Flood slowly coming back to the God he had resented for so many decades. And through the very life—and death—of Aggie's mother, Jesus fulfilled his promise from John 12:24:

> "I tell you the truth, unless a kernel of wheat is planted in
> the soil and dies, it remains alone.
> But its death will produce many new kernels—
> a plentiful harvest of new lives" (NLT).

QUESTIONS FROM SINGLES

The people in this actual missionary-life story suffered a deeper family tragedy than most other missionaries ever experience. But accompanying the heart-tugging trials that both singles and couples face in God's global mission story are many miraculous and amazing eternity-changing events.

Let's begin this chapter by talking through some of the realities, practicalities, and benefits of serving in missions as a single person.

Q. What perspective should I take toward serving in missions as a single person?

A: Both singleness and marriage have rewards and challenges; either way, God promises us his help and presence.

When considering the benefits of working as a single person in missions, we need to recognize that the apostle Paul encouraged singleness: "He who refrains from marriage will do even better" (1 Corinthians 7:38 ESV). Missionary statesman John Stott opted for singleness in order to give himself more fully to the ministry. To him, this was a personal direction from the Lord, but not a pattern for all. Viv Grigg, led to minister in the slums, noted the difficulty of raising a family in such a context.

When considering the benefits of working as a married missionary, the majority of those would undoubtedly testify of the incredible blessing of being married and raising a family in another culture. Also, the practices of biblical marriage and child rearing need to be modeled. Paul's command for husbands to love their wives and wives to respect their husbands is a universal command that fits into any culture. My wife, Mary Anne, and I lived for seventeen years on the second floor of a student center in Bogotá, Colombia. We prayed that our relationship as husband and wife and as a family would be positive illustrations to the students.

For single women desiring to marry, mission-field living poses a statistical challenge: single women who remain on the mission field usually don't marry because there are so few single men to even meet and because single men typically marry in their first few years overseas.

One way to face this issue of singleness is through God's sovereignty. The God who calls us to follow him promises to us his presence ("I will never leave you nor forsake you," Joshua 1:5) and to supply our needs ("My God will meet all your needs," Philippians 4:19). He does not, however, promise us a spouse. But if he considers that a spouse is truly our need, he is well able to supply us with one.

Answer from Jack Voelkel, missionary-in-residence with the Urbana Student Mission Convention. Previously Jack served for thirty years with Latin America Mission in Peru and Colombia.

A. Surrender to God your desire for marriage; then trust his plan for you.

I was afraid that I would not meet anyone I could marry and that I would remain single if I stayed overseas for any length of time. I wrestled with this issue and finally read a book that I knew about but had been avoiding, *Single and Satisfied*. I was not sure I wanted to be satisfied with being single! But reading it did the trick. I became convinced that if God wanted me to be single, he would be all that I needed and I would be satisfied. On the other hand, if God did have a husband in my plan, he would bring about our meeting, and I didn't need to worry about it. Given where I would be serving, I figured that the latter was highly unlikely, so I surrendered to God my desire to marry, which had been strong since I was a young girl. I would go, even if it meant remaining single.

Three weeks after that, I met a young, single missionary named Jerry at a planning meeting for a high school outreach. This event would feature our singing group in a camp setting, and Jerry was on the camp board. He had been serving in Korea for a number of years. When we met, we discovered our mutual love for the Lord and desire to serve in Korea. We immediately recognized that God had brought us together. We found that as we were each following God's plan individually, his plan for us to serve together in Korea as a married couple came together.[1]

Answer from Barb, who served with Operation Mobilization in South Korea.

A: Single missionaries have more flexibility to immerse in a culture.

From my experience, serving as a single person in missions is great. Why? I get to bond with the culture in incredible ways. For example, I lived with a local family for my first six months in ministry, and I became their "daughter," attending every family event and holiday. Our singleness allows us the flexibility and mobility to dive deeply into the culture.

Answer from Melinda, who has served for nine years in a ministry to Muslims, with five years working in Central Asia.

A: Singles can focus solely on serving God.

Mission service is different from a job. It's a *lifestyle* lived every day, night, weekend, and holiday. It's a culture in itself. In that culture of ministry, we should understand that, as single women, we are free to serve God *above all*.

If we choose to marry, we lose that focused attention as we become wives. We may be the same people, but our ministry has changed from serving others to serving our husbands. That's not a bad thing. In fact, it's a great honor. But it is an extreme change for a woman in missions.

Also, make certain you and your dream man have the same vision *before* you commit to a life that is not for you. Pray diligently about the matter, because if you're an unhappy wife you will hinder the ministry of your husband and of missions.

If you choose to marry, serve your husband with all you have and do it joyfully. If you don't marry, serve God with all your might.

Answer from Jessie, a single woman who has served for four years in Mexico.

Q: Should I, as a single person, go overseas now, or should I first find a mate?

A: Go as a single, knowing God himself will supply your needs.

I struggled with this issue. I didn't want to go into missions as a single, so I decided to find a mate before going. But then someone told me that if I wanted to find a man who was committed to missions, I should look for him overseas, which made a lot of sense. After all, if he's obedient to the Lord, then he's already there, not at home. Right?

So I finally decided to go overseas. Mostly it's great, and I don't mind being single. But there are times when what's ahead seems daunting, and a partner to help pursue the vision would be great. But I trust the Lord. He knows whether I can better do what he's leading me to do with a partner or without one. And I believe he will equip me with whatever I need. Look to him alone for your fulfillment.

Answer from Monica, who has served for two years with Youth With A Mission.

A: Get on God's path for you; then trust him for your future.

Sometimes we forget that the God who leads us into missions also has our future planned. The biggest tools of a successful missionary are trust and faith in God. Trusting him with your love life is a great way to start.

Knowing I was going into missions, I graduated from Bible school. I also knew that the Great Commission was clear. So although I wanted to get married, I went to Honduras as a full-time missionary.

I found the man God had for me when I got on the *path* God had for me. He was serving in the same ministry. We met in Honduras and were married there. That was eight years ago. I am still here, serving the Lord with all my heart alongside the man God sent to me as I took the steps to obey and trust his path.

Answer from Kimberly, who has served for ten years in Honduras.

A: Obey God's leading and go.

I determined a few years ago that, since God was leading me into missions, first, I must obey, and second, as I obeyed he would bring along someone with the same passion, working in the same part of the world.

Trust God. If he led you into missions and wants you married, he will cause your two paths to merge into one. You will have a *much* happier marriage than if you stay in your home country and marry someone who does not share that vision.

Answer from Heather, who serves in the Ukraine as a career missionary with the Assemblies of God.

A: Get moving, keep your eyes open, and don't limit God.

My wife and I met overseas and married a year later. The biggest dilemma single missionaries talk about is whether God has directed them to stay single. When I left for East Asia, I was twenty-five years old. Many people close to me strongly questioned my decision, since I was single. But I decided to follow God first and continue trusting him for a wife.

In light of my experience, I offer the following three pieces of advice:

1. Get moving toward missions without waiting around to get married. God will honor your faithfulness and bless you greatly in every way.
2. Keep your eyes open for potential spouses. If you feel that God has not directed you to stay single, then neither give up on getting married nor stop looking.
3. Single missionaries often overlook potential love interests based on a petty, limited perspective about how perfect their potential spouse needs to be. We all have deficiencies that God works out as we grow in marriage. I know of several single men on the field who were a little quirky but were radically transformed through the tender hand of a loving wife. Don't limit God by overlooking his perfect choice for you because of small things that don't really matter.

Having dated on the mission field, I have one final piece of advice for single missionaries. Dating can feel as if you're in a small town, with everybody having his or her own special opinion about your relationship. The pastor who eventually married us gave us this great advice: "Find one mature couple you trust and can confide in; then tell everyone else to mind their own business."

Answer from Kyle, a missionary with Pioneers, serving with his wife and two children in Asia.

Q. Should I consider a relationship with a future missionary who wants to serve in a country different from where I'm interested?

A: Yes, but work toward a common vision.

Don't abandon someone just because they want to go to a different part of the world. Search for a reasonable compromise. Maybe you both should take the time and money to visit the parts of the world in which you each are interested. The fact that you both want to go overseas is already a good reason to seek what God might have for you together.

Answer from Mike, who served ten years in West Africa and North Africa on a Bible translation team with WEC International.

A: Only if you can commit wholeheartedly to your spouse.

Before I married, I was determined that God wanted me to go to Japan. In fact, before I married Susan, I told her more than once that if I had to choose between marrying her and going to Japan, I would go to Japan. (She envisioned being a missionary but had never seriously considered Japan.)

However, since getting married, I have come to realize the importance of my vow and responsibility to Susan according to God's Word. Now, if I ever have to choose between staying in Japan and protecting my marriage and family, I would choose to protect my family.

In short, marriage should resemble the self-sacrificing love Christ has for his church; anything less does little good for the cause of Christ. If you're not ready for such a commitment, it is better not to marry.

Answer from John, who has served in Japan for nine years with SEND International.

Q : How do singles living overseas . deal with loneliness and isolation?

A : Enjoy time alone with God and intentionally . build same-sex friendships.

Loneliness comes in many forms. The answer is to look to the Lord who promises to be *everything* we need. It's so good when we can rejoice in seasons of time alone with our Father. But he surely created us to also be in community at times, so being intentional about building relationships is critical.

In a new place, it's an easy trap to think that you are the only one who doesn't fit in, that everyone else is already set in a group, and that there is no room for you. Those are lies. God has gone before you to provide people to love you and to care for you as you care for others. Continue seeking his face first, and then look for those women (if you are female) who may be used of God to care for you.

I strongly recommend against finding men for this role, even father-figure type men. A more seasoned missionary once cautioned me, "No matter what the man calls you, sister, daughter, or friend, he still sees you as a woman."

Answer from Catherine, who has served with SEND for two years in Alaska.

A : Be intentional about building family-type . relationships.

The most important thing I've learned about being single is that I still *need* family. It takes time and effort to build close-knit relationships with others to the point where you really feel part of a family. You have to prioritize time to spend with those who are becoming your family, just as married couples have to prioritize time together and with their children. Sacrifices will need to be made, but the intimacy of being known and belonging will have life-saving benefits.

The challenge of building such deep relationships with other missionaries or nationals is that, at some point, your paths will part . . . and the separation will be painful. But again, the pain of losing close relationships is worth the joy and security you will have experienced while you were together.

As for isolation, if you are the type of person who needs close relationships and regular social interaction, do not choose to go to a place where you will live isolated from people with whom you could build friendships. It takes a special type of personality to thrive and remain healthy in a lonesome environment.

Answer from Lisa, who has served with International Teams for twenty-one years in Austria, Romania, and Canada.

APPREHENSIVE PARENTS OR GRANDPARENTS

Consider this startling reality: Becoming a missionary is not always a popular decision. Prospective missionaries, whether single or married, young or old, will face some degree of opposition from someone they care about.

If this disapproval comes from a mother or a father, the emotional challenges can be extremely difficult to handle. But once again, the God who calls us into missions is fully ready to counsel and guide our parents and us through the challenges of this major life decision. With patient wisdom, let's hear the thoughtful ideas of missionaries who have faced the opposition of apprehensive parents.

Q. What if a parent opposes me becoming a missionary?

A: Help them see the positive side of missions.

Ask God to guide you, to change your parents' hearts, and to bring into their lives people who would positively influence them toward missions.

Maybe they think you're destined to a life of poverty. They need to be exposed to the positive side of missionary work. Invite missionaries home to a meal, or invite your parents to hear missionaries speak at church.

Be willing to wait before you actually go long term. From time to time, talk casually about your desire to be a missionary, which will help the idea sink in a bit. And approach your future in small steps—go first on a local mission trip and then on an overseas mission trip.

Answer from Jennifer, serving in West Africa with United World Mission.

A: Be patient and watch God change their hearts.

When I found out that I would have to make a two-year commitment to the mission field, my immediate reaction was, *Forget it! I won't quit my job for that. My job is too good to give up. Besides, what would my dad, who paid for my studies for seven years, say?*

I had only been working for three years. He is not a Christian and would probably think that he invested his money in vain. I especially thought he wouldn't like the fact that I needed to raise support, because he values independence.

I decided to go on the mission field eighteen months later. This time of waiting gave my family a chance to get used to the fact that I would be leaving for two years. I was surprised that my father did not react as I expected. He had no problem with me quitting my job. He thought it would be good for me to see the world and that I would learn a lot. It was harder for my mother to accept because she has such different beliefs and does not understand how I can travel around to promote the Bible. But she changed her mind once she visited the ministry and saw that we offer the gospel only to those who are looking for the truth. She actually has become quite positive about it as she tells other about what I am doing.[2]

Answer from Barbel, who serves with Operation Mobilization.

A: God can care for your parents as you obey him.

Both my wife and I are first generation Christians, so when we became interested in missions, we had opposition from both our families. In our case, we heard from the Lord an assurance that if we were about his business, he would take care of ours.

Our four parents did come to Jesus, and we were in America when each died. They were happy we served in missions.

It may be helpful to know that many agencies, including WEC, allow their missionaries to take an extended leave of absence to care for aging parents at home.

Answer from David Smith, director of mobilization with WEC International. David has been a missionary for twenty-five years as a field worker in West Africa and at WEC USA headquarters.

A: Connect with the National Network of Parents of Missionaries.

Disapproving parents keep many young people off the mission field. Many others who do go overseas leave behind parents who are supportive but hurting. Missionaries, recruits, and their parents can find understanding and helpful support through the book *Parents of Missionaries* and the National Network of Parents of Missionaries (see "Resources for Further Study").

DISINTERESTED SPOUSES

You may be the spouse who *does not* want to serve in missions, or your spouse may be the disinterested one while you feel it's God's plan. Either way, both views must be considered and even respected. Remember that God is able to accomplish his plans in us, through us, and, sometimes, in spite of us—whether his plan is to go or to stay.

A wise church leader can counsel and guide couples in processing their differences related to mission service. Let's consider some of the objections and fears a disinterested spouse might have.

Q: I want to be a missionary, but my spouse does not. How have other married couples resolved their differing desires?

A. If it's God's plan, he will work out each concern.

When I married Chuck, I knew there was a strong likelihood that we would go overseas, because he had been to Yugoslavia, had loved it there, and wanted to go back. I knew I did not want to go there, or anywhere else, but I knew I was opening the door to this possibility by marrying him. My main obstacle then was thinking that I would have to attend Bible school. I also really wanted children, and we were in the process of beginning a domestic adoption, which is a long, involved process. I also knew that neither of our families would want us to go, as neither were believers and no one would want their first grandchild to be out of the country. I basically got cold feet about going overseas, and we stopped the process.

What was I afraid of? Many things: that I wouldn't be able to handle it, that I'd go nuts, and that I wouldn't be able to adopt a second child.

Seven years later, God opened a door for us to take a short-term trip to Central Asia. Even then, I knew we would be returning there to live, but I did not want to go. I began to cry. Finally, Chuck wrestled with God and made the life-changing decision that we would go overseas even if we had to raise support. I agreed. I couldn't believe myself! I had come full circle on the issue, and I knew this was one more obstacle in which the Lord wanted me to trust him.

Then there was the issue of our parents. Neither of our parents were believers, nor were the rest of our immediate families. We had two boys and the only grandchildren on either side. We knew that both sets of parents would be against our going, but God worked even that out. Even though our parents did not really want us to go overseas, they did not make a big fuss. They were as supportive as they could be, even though they would miss the boys and us greatly and worry a lot to boot.[3]

Answer from Stacy, who serves in Central Asia with Operation Mobilization.

A. There are many ways couples can serve together; but both spouses must be led to overseas missions.

We decided early in our mission involvement that any commitment to overseas missions should be a 100 percent call to both of us as a married couple. There are too many other stresses in overseas service; to have a half-committed partner would be a real problem. For one spouse to go only because the other feels called will likely not result in an effective ministry.

There are other ways in which a couple can serve in missions—on your church mission board, going on or leading short-term teams, supporting missionaries financially, hosting missionaries and foreign visitors in your home, or being involved with organizations such as Wycliffe Associates or others who rely heavily on home-based membership. These activities might even lead the reluctant spouse into overseas service.

Answer from Craig, who serves in Papua New Guinea with Wycliffe Bible Translators.

SMALL CHILDREN IN A BIG WORLD

Two enemy villages in Irian Jaya had vowed to destroy each other, until a missionary couple presented their infant son as the mutual "peace child." The ceremony amazingly prevented a war. This story alone makes for a good book and an uplifting movie. But there's more. Decades later, that same "peace child"—Steve Richardson—is father to his own children and provides leadership to missionary families of the mission agency Pioneers.

Your family's mission story may be less dramatic than that of the Richardson family. But the God who affected a village and a world through these missionary parents and their child is the same God who can be trusted with your family.

Let's learn from experienced missionary parents the joys and benefits of having their small children somewhere in the big world.

Q: Can a couple with small children make it to the mission field?

A: Yes. It's easier to go when your kids are young.

I grew up as a missionary kid in Palestine and Egypt, and I wouldn't exchange my mission experiences for the world. My kids have also moved a lot, and they feel the same.

Although small children will need care and one of you will likely have to devote a good bit of time to them, it's widely accepted in some cultures to employ a nanny. This can help free mom for quality time with the kids as well as help the kids to adjust in the new culture.

Younger is better in terms of a family's adjustment to cross-cultural missions. The earlier your kids accept the host culture as their own home and learn the language, the easier their adjustment will be.

As wonderful as it is to visit your home country and grandparents, I encourage grandparents to visit you during the first two or three years. A minimum three-year commitment makes the new home real.

Answer from Elizabeth, a missionary mom who has served in India and China.

A: Yes. Children can open the hearts of hard-to-reach people.

We took our two kids to the mission field of West Africa when they were very young. It is highly possible to be effective missionaries with a growing family—my parents did it with five kids.

Families often have advantages that single missionaries don't have. For example, through our children, we can more easily interact with another culture. The people most resistant to the gospel can be open to interacting with missionary families.

Stay focused on the high calling of missions. The needs are great and the stakes are high, but the rewards are limitless.

Answer from Dick, who served with Serving In Mission (SIM) in Nigeria for thirteen years.

A: Yes. Missionary kids are more likely to succeed.

The answer is a big yes. Not only can a couple make it to the field with small children, I am sure they can also thrive there. Let me explain.

I went into missions with a wife, a two-month-old baby, and an eighteen-month-old toddler. With two in diapers, we had many concerns. But I've learned that God uses families. Our children opened doors of ministry for us—after all, everyone likes a baby. All true ministry to others flows out of what is happening at home.

I've read that one of every eight missionary children makes the list of *Who's Who in America*. Contrast this number with about one of one hundred thousand nonmissionary American children. All three of my children were blessed by growing up in another culture. They are bicultural and multilingual, they have people skills, and they are musicians. And all three are in *Who's Who in America*.

Answer from Dale Pugh, international Coordinator of World International Mission, who served long term in Mexico.

A: Yes. Consider these benefits of going now.

With such a broad spectrum of mission scenarios, it's hard to generalize. As with any family, much depends on your job as parents as well as the specific place where you serve. There are, however, many benefits to going when your children are young, including these:

1. Your family is young and adaptable.
2. It's easier for all of you to learn a foreign language.
3. The more comfortable you get at home, and the more your family patterns are set, the harder it is to make a major move.
4. Having babies is a worldwide experience. In most countries, there are adequate facilities, unless there are complications. I was born in Pyong Yang, Korea.

Answer from Jack Voelkel.

THE ABCs OF SCHOOLING OPTIONS

Q: If we move overseas, what do we do about our children's education?

A: Examine all the options with your mission agency.

WEC has nearly two thousand missionaries and approximately the same number of missionary kids, so educating children is an issue we deal with constantly. Our general policy is that parents make the education decision in consultation with field leaders. The only real condition we set is that over time the choice has to show itself to be effective for the individual child.

Many of our families send their children to *national schools*. This is most true in Europe. Many other countries have *international schools,* which have high academic standards and a price tag to match. *Schools for missionary kids,* another education option, often serve missionary children from several missions and even several countries.

Many families *home school* for the earliest years, but most eventually opt for another program when the children grow older, for two reasons. First, home schooling becomes difficult and demanding for the parents, who see themselves as missionaries as well as parents. Second, parents recognize that the social needs of children are often met in schools, especially schools specifically for missionary children, where a positive peer pressure is generally provided in a spiritual setting.

A study published in *Evangelical Missions Quarterly* showed that the children of missionaries were better prepared educationally, socially, spiritually, and emotionally than were the other children in the study. That's encouraging.

Of course, real answers will come as you select a mission agency, which will have specific education guidelines. Other answers may come as you examine a possible assignment. For example, a certain area may have limited options for educating children. One thing of which you can be certain is that God cares as much for your children as he does for any person in the world.

Answer from David Smith, director of mobilization with WEC International. David has been a missionary for twenty-five years as a field worker in West Africa and at WEC USA headquarters.

A: Consider the pros and cons of these four schooling options.

There are four major options to consider for your child's education. My wife and I have talked and prayed and struggled over the best course of education for our children (now ages nine, seven, and two) and will probably continue to do so as they grow. Four options we've considered include the following:

1. *National school*. Many missionaries in Japan, but probably not the majority, send their children to public school, especially for elementary grades. We sent our boys to a Japanese preschool and kindergarten.

2. *Mission school or school for foreigners*. This option is, of course, limited to those areas where such a school exists, and these schools may be expensive. In Japan there are several mission schools in or near large cities.

3. *Boarding school*. If a mission school is not available, another option is a boarding school (or a school where your children can board with trusted family or friends). This may be a school in the nation where you serve or farther away. Some parents even send their children to live with friends or relatives in their home country (usually only for high school).

4. *Home school*. With increasing amounts of material available, home school is becoming a commonly used education option. Similar to home school, a team or group of missionaries could create a small school where parents take various responsibilities in teaching. Another option is for the mission agency to provide a teacher for the group.

All of the options above have both pros and cons. The final decision will rest with each family, depending on finances, options available, convictions, personalities, and needs of the children. No matter which course you choose, your children will be third-culture children with the accompanying special needs and benefits.

Answer from John, who has served in Japan for seven years with TTW/Hi-BA.

A: Consider different options at different ages.

Our son was five when we arrived in Slovakia. Right away, we put him in a Slovak kindergarten, and he loved it from day one (being an only child may have helped). He acquired the language quite rapidly—though his parents were much slower!

He is now in seventh grade, attending a Slovak public school (the only kind of school he has ever attended). Slovaks place a much higher value on math and science than Americans do, so he has already studied physics and algebra.

We spend every second summer in America, which hasn't been a problem, though Slovak schools end June 30 and begin September 4. Our son enjoys missing that last month of school. He recently decided that he would like to attend an MK (missionary kid) boarding school his final two years of high school so that he can develop some Christian friendships.

Answer from Tom, who has served for seven years in Slovakia with Campus Crusade for Christ.

A: Remember that kids are resilient.

I was raised for fifteen years in northern Brazil. I attended first and second grade in an English-language school; the rest of my education was either from home school or correspondence courses. My home school was based on books we had in the house, much as kids on the American frontier learned.

My boys attend a Spanish-language school here in Colombia. We pay the tuition for this private school because of the frequent strikes that interrupt the public school year. Tuition is inexpensive here—only about fifty dollars a month per child, plus books and uniforms. Our children are getting a good education, perhaps even better than they would in many places at home, and they're learning more of the language and culture in which they live. We speak English in the house, and we tutor them in English to keep up their reading skills.

Don't let kid worries keep you off the mission field. Kids are resilient.

Answer from Paul in Colombia, who has served fourteen years as a missionary.

A: Consider an agency's values on education before joining.

As you examine various mission agencies, balance their values on schooling against your own. Some agencies consider the parents' missionary work to be the priority—so parents must send their kids to boarding school when they turn six years old. Other agencies let parents make schooling decisions.

Some common choices for schooling missionary kids include home school and the local school. My assistant Paul, who grew up overseas, attended a neighborhood school. He never knows how to answer the question, "What was it like to attend school overseas?" He says it's no different from school anywhere—some things are fun, and some things aren't. To get an idea of how missionary kids live, visit mukappa.org.

Answer from Jack Voelkel.

RESISTANCE FROM OLDER CHILDREN

Q: What if my teenage kids don't want to move to the mission field?

A: Put your teens first.

Principle 1: Being a successful missionary but a failure as a parent is not an option.

Principle 2: If it's God's will for you to be overseas, it's God's will for your kids to be there too.

Others can give you advice, but be certain your call to launch into missions now is not motivated by anything other than God's will. If your kids are resisting, it could be that God is using them to check your motives and timing.

If they don't want to go with you, don't risk making them bitter for the rest of their lives just to do something you want to do. If they are opposed to going with you, I advise waiting until they are on their own and have a good support system in place before you leave for your mission assignment.

Answer from Char, who has served nineteen years in Guatemala, South Korea, China, and Africa.

Q: Can I become a missionary if my adult children still need me nearby?

A: Maybe yes, maybe no.

This depends on several factors. If your children are dependent on you financially, spiritually, emotionally, or physically, then it may not be a good time to consider such a move. Look for God's confirmation to come through your adult children as well as your pastor.

Before we seriously considered missions, we shared this possibility with our children, who were ages 18, 20, 23, and 24 at the time. None were married, and two were in university. We could not have made the move without their full and unconditional support. During the past eight years, it's been possible for us to come home to participate in weddings, in the births of our grandchildren, and in graduations. Yes, this has come at a cost both in finances and in schedule planning.

Some voiced concerns that our moving so far from home would sever future contact. The opposite has been true. Since we have the need and the desire to phone, our relationships have deepened.

At a time when we were experiencing loneliness for our children, we received this promise from God: "As much as you miss each other, pray for your children and know that your loneliness is only a fraction of mine for you when you are not close to me." God will teach you how to make your together times special and to solidify your relationships as you depend wholly on him.

Answer from Jerry and Robin, who have been missionaries in Japan for eight years.

MY THOUGHTS SO FAR

On-the-field missionaries need to regularly talk and pray with friends, prayer partners, and counselors about being single, about being married, or about raising children in the practicalities of mission life. Even before committing to a life of mission service, it's a good idea to get the input of a leader in your local church on this chapter's questions. As you answer the relevant questions, ask the Holy Spirit to guide you, through God's Word and through prayer. Answer each question in light of what you *currently* understand from God.

QUESTIONS FOR SINGLES

What are my perspectives, both positive and negative, toward serving in missions as a single person?

_____

_____

_____

How can I correct my negative perspectives and attitudes?

_____

_____

_____

Should I go overseas first, or should I find a mate first? What leading in this area have I received from God?

_____

_____

_____

How would I deal with loneliness and isolation while living overseas?

_____

_____

_____

QUESTIONS FOR COUPLES

What issues do we have about going into missions as a couple? How can we work through them?

_____

_____

_____

_____

I want to be a missionary, but my spouse does not. How can we resolve our differing desires?

_____

_____

_____

In what ways could we help our children, whether young or grown, deal with us moving overseas?

_____

_____

_____

_____

What are our thoughts on the best schooling options for our smaller children?

_____

_____

_____

GENERAL QUESTIONS

How can I help my mother and father prepare for my life as a missionary?

_____

_____

_____

Both single and married women serving in missions encounter a unique set of challenges. Preparing for these challenges is critical. From the books and newsletters listed in "Resources for Further Study," select two resources on women in missions to investigate further:

1. _____

_____

2. _____

_____

THE CHALLENGE
Moving Forward

7

DR. GIBSON AND I EASED INTO THE BAMBOO CHAIRS on the veranda of a local missionary's home. I mentioned how profoundly thankful I was to be back on the coast and off the dusty interior roads of Papua New Guinea.

"Dr. Gibson, today you talked about overcoming the obstacle of fear, something about your Thailand days as a missionary?"

And with that simple inquiry, Dr. Gibson launched into one of his richly wise stories.

"After years of running a mission hospital in central Thailand, I moved north into a remote province—near the border with Laos. We opened a clinic and took mobile-medical trips to serve the needs of unreached tribes.

"On a medical trip, we would treat an entire village. We gave free medicine for typical ailments. We met with village leadership. And after dark we showed the *JESUS* film. These medical trips opened villages to evangelism and church planting.

"Then a church planter named Phil asked me to hold mobile clinics in another province of Thailand about a hundred kilometers away, a region where we hadn't worked. Phil worked with a people group living in that province and into the neighboring country. Almost everyone working with that people group worked in stealth mode. In closed countries or hostile cultures, some missionaries say that they work in business or in medicine or in education and don't reveal their missionary intentions.

"But in our province, we had been forthright about our work. We developed an open relationship with the governor, health officials, and local government leaders. We always asked their permission and advice before moving into a new area or holding a mobile clinic. So, as usual, I sent documents to the governor of Phil's target province. I simply described the medical clinic work and our intent to work in his province, if it were agreeable.

"Phil was pretty nervous when, two weeks later, we got a phone call from that province's governor, telling us to report to his office and explain our intentions. Three days after the call, Phil, one of our Thai Christian leaders, and I bounced across miles and miles of jungle roads to pay what I expected to be a normal ceremonial visit to the governor.

"We arrived at the governor's office after hours of sweltering travel. I was somewhat surprised when we were asked to wait outside his office, which was unusual when compared with the normal reception from hospitality-conscious Thai officials. After nearly an hour, a military guard appeared and directed us through large double doors into the gloom of the governor's office.

"The governor sat behind his desk, staring at a sheaf of documents. He didn't even look up. So the three of us just stood there, awkward and suddenly very nervous.

"Without a greeting, without looking at us, he growled, 'You people are missionaries who want to convert these people, are you not?'

"My heart bounded into my throat, and my stealth-mode

missionary friend Phil almost choked. I was tempted to tell the governor about our humanitarian motives, our medical works, our development projects, our cooperation within the government system. But it was as if the truth had to burst out of my mouth. 'Yes, sir. Our desire is to share the love of Jesus Christ through medical care.'

"Dead silence. Then he glanced up from his papers, looked me eye-to-eye—and burst into laughter. I almost had a heart attack. He stood up, still laughing, and said, 'That was my test of you. I've already checked with the provincial governors where you have previously worked. I wanted to see if you would be honest with me and admit your actual motives.'

"Then he sat in his executive chair and happily asked us to tell him about other projects we'd done in Thailand. So we told him about our HIV/AIDS ministry, our drug rehab programs, and the medical teaching we offer. With all of us breathing again, we had a marvelous conversation on why Jesus Christ is bringing health and hope to the Thai, which means 'the free.'

"Finally, the governor took out his pen, signed his name at the bottom of the mobile-clinic proposal, and added a note: 'Whatever Dr. Gibson wants to do in this province, he has the permission of the governor.' Then he called the head of public health and instructed her to help with logistic or hospitality needs we might have in his province."

In the darkening evening, the good doctor in turn asked me a simple question. "What does that story from Thailand suggest to you as you explore your part in God's global plan?"

I scratched my head. "Well, I think of 2 Timothy something . . . 'For God did not give us a spirit of timidity, but a spirit of power, of love and of self-discipline.'"

Dr. Gibson smiled in the yellow glow of the bug light on the veranda. "Chapter one, verse seven—an excellent application. You're exploring an unknown future in missions, right? Well, during uncertain times, Christ's followers never need to surrender to fear. Why? Because God himself is our certain reality. In his power, we can fearlessly and calmly move forward, confident that he not only knows the way but that he also goes before us. So be encouraged in your exploration process. God is with you."

POWER THAT OVERCOMES FEAR

Some people wrongly assume that missionaries have no fear. In this chapter's opening story, however, Dr. Gibson reminds us that Christ's followers, missionaries included, can be intimidated—especially in unknown situations. With still unanswered questions and unresolved dilemmas about becoming a missionary, you too could certainly feel that you're walking an unsure path with little light for the way.

So how can we move forward through the unknowns and challenges of cross-cultural service rather than giving up in fear? According to 2 Timothy 1:7, we can exchange a "spirit of timidity" for a "spirit of power." That is, we trade our fear for trust in the perfect love of a God for whom nothing is unknown.

Moving forward in obedience to God, especially when the path is dark, *always* strengthens our reliance on and trust in him—vital qualities for cross-cultural missionaries. As Isaiah suggests, "Who among you fears the LORD and obeys the word of his servant? Let him who walks in the dark, who has no light, trust in the name of the LORD and rely on his God (50:10)."

So as you consider becoming a missionary, invite God's power to overcome fear of the unknown as he walks you through the challenges of mission service, challenges such as these:

- *Discovering God's guidance*. Whether you're already moving forward into missions or you're waiting on God for further guidance, you won't have complete answers to every question. Depend not on your own wisdom, but on the Lord's power to guide you step by step (Proverbs 3:5–6).

- *Finding the right agency and place*. Perhaps you feel overwhelmed by the number of mission opportunities and organizations, wondering how you could ever sort through it all. Trust God to guide you in his time to the agency and place he has prepared for you.

- *Getting the right training*. There are many options for mission training. Get what you need now, and trust the Lord to teach you more when you need it.

- *Figuring out funding details*. Recall the times God has allowed uncomfortable circumstances in your life—for your spiritual and personal growth. Raising prayer and financial support may be a similarly uncomfortable step God has planned for you. Learn to trust our faithful God to work for your good in uncomfortable circumstances.

- *Counting the relational cost of mission service:* Most singles have concerns about going into mission service unmarried. And most parents have some fears for their children's health and education in another culture. Father God knows your concerns and fears, and he *will* care for you and for yours as you serve him.

As you explore your role in God's mission story, remember to utilize some of the invaluable resources for further study listed at the end of this book. Discuss issues and questions with a leader or friend in your local church. Ask the Holy Spirit to guide you, through God's Word and through prayer. Invite God's power to overcome your fears and concerns. With complete confidence in his power, move forward as he guides.

As you grow closer to the Lord of the harvest, never rely on your own insight or understanding, but instead, "trust in the name of the LORD and rely on [your] God" (Isaiah 50:10).

ACKNOWLEDGMENTS

The editor, John McVay, wants to express deep appreciation to those who made this book possible:

- The one hundred missionaries who contributed valuable answers to a multitude of questions.
- William (Bill) Stearns for researching and writing chapter one as well as the dynamic stories that open each chapter.
- Volney James, John Dunham, and Andy Sloan at Authentic Publishing for shaping this into a better book than I thought possible.
- Dana Bromley, for her diligent editing that has transformed a rough manuscript into an organized and useful book.
- Nate Wilson, Mike B., and David Smith for their encouragement and partnership in the beginning of Ask A Missionary in 1999 with the first e-newsletters.
- Mark Orr for programming in 2000 the first version of AskAMissionary.com, and Tim Williston for the amazing upgrades he developed between 2005 and 2008.
- Peter Armstrong, Hannah Nielsen, and the M-DAT team for revamping and running

AskAMissionary.com since 2009.

- Lindsay Goodier for editing hundreds of online answers, and Dave Imboden for helping develop the section "Resources for Further Study."

- The leaders and missionaries from TCF, Carbondale and In His Image who have coached me in missions and in serving God.

- My colleagues at The Journey Deepens retreats—Dave Leggett, Mike Eager, Steve Hoke, John and Jamie Zumwalt, Don and Ele Parrott—for your partnership in mission mobilization.

- My friends Dave Mason, Gene McMath, Ric Shields. My mentors Bruce Clutter, Jim Garrett, Ben Dodwell. My co-workers at In His Image Family Medicine Residency and Medical Missions. My children—Michelle, Brian and Roxana, Mark, David, Annie, Bethany. Thank you all for your love, encouragement, and prayer support.

- My lovely wife, Nicole, thank you for 26 amazing years of marriage and all your sacrifices for me, for our children, and for missions. I treasure you as my beauty, my joy, and my partner in serving Jesus.

Lord of the harvest, thank you
for allowing me to join you in mobilizing future
missionaries.
"May all the peoples praise you" (Psalm 67).

NOTES

CHAPTER 2: GUIDANCE

1. Excerpt from *Screams in the Desert* by Sue Eenigenburg (William Carey Library, 2007).
2. Excerpt adapted from *Scaling the Wall: Overcoming Obstacles to Missions Involvement* by Kathy Hicks (Authentic, 2003), 68–72.

CHAPTER 3: AGENCIES

1. Excerpt from "We Found That We Needed Agencies," in *Mobilizer* (Advancing Churches in Missions Commitment, March 2002).

CHAPTER 4: TRAINING

1. Excerpt from *Brigada,* a free, global e-newsletter published by Doug Lucas of Team Expansion.
2. Excerpt from *On Being a Missionary: A Complete Look at What It Takes* by Thomas Hale (William Carey Library, 1995), 30ff.
3. Excerpt from *Scaling the Wall: Overcoming Obstacles to Missions Involvement* by Kathy Hicks (Authentic, 2003), 173.
4. Excerpt from *Global Mission Handbook: A Guide for Crosscultural Service* by Steve Hoke and Bill Taylor (IVP, 2009).
5. Excerpt from *Scaling the Wall: Overcoming Obstacles to Missions Involvement* by Kathy Hicks (Authentic, 2003), 168.
6. Excerpt from *On Being a Missionary: A Complete Look at What It Takes* by Thomas Hale (William Carey Library, 1995), 30ff.

CHAPTER 5: FUNDING

1. Excerpt from *Müller of Bristol* by Arthur T. Pierson (Fleming Revell), 448.
2. Excerpt from *Delighted in God* by Roger Steer (OMF), 221.
3. Excerpt from the Larry Burkett radio show *Money Matters* that aired on February 3, 1999.

CHAPTER 6: SINGLES, COUPLES, AND KIDS

1. Excerpt from *Scaling the Wall: Overcoming Obstacles to Missions Involvement* by Kathy Hicks (Authentic, 2003), 105.
2. Ibid., 57.
3. Ibid., 77.

RESOURCES FOR FURTHER STUDY

These mission-related resources for further study include organizations, books, websites, magazines, courses, events, and specific support in missions for you and your church. Browse TheJourneyDeepens.com > Global Mission Resources for online updates to this list.

NEXT STEPS INTO MISSIONS

Finishers.org

Information and pathways for adults considering a second-half career in missions.

GoConnect.org/nextsteps

Resources for many strategic roles in missions: senders, goers, givers, "gray-ers," welcomers, mobilizers, and networkers.

Perspectives.org > Next Steps

A resource center for alumni of the Perspectives course.

PreparingToGo.com

A resource center for aspiring missionaries.

TheJourneyDeepens.com

Weekend retreats for prospective missionaries.

Urbana.org > Next Steps

Resources and opportunities for students to be involved in God's kingdom work.

MISSION OPPORTUNITIES AROUND THE WORLD

Finishers.org

Database service that matches mission-agency openings to a person's skills, experience, and ministry preferences.

MissionFinder.org

Classified directory of Christian-mission opportunities by agency name.

MNNonline.org > Mission Trips

Connects individuals and groups of all ages with a mission opportunity.

RightNow.org

Counsel and database to connect young adults with service opportunities.

ServantOpportunities.net

Database of both volunteer and career opportunities for midlifers and older adults.

ShortTermMissions.com

Database helps all ages connect with a mission opportunity, from one week to three years, that fits their gifts and calling.

Urbana.org > MSearch

Connects students with organizations for service opportunities and training in cross-cultural ministry.

MISSION EVENTS AROUND THE WORLD

Brigada.org

Weekly e-newsletter announcing upcoming mission events

around the world, new resources, and mission-related courses.

MissionEventsCalendar.com

Lists upcoming mission events in North America.

GoConnect.org/conferences

Calendar for short-term and missionary-candidate training events as well as mission conferences, seminars, and courses.

Oscar.org.uk > News and Events

Lists upcoming mission events in the United Kingdom and around the world.

Q&A AND SUPPORT IN MISSIONS

AskAMissionary.com

Gives over four hundred answers to questions on becoming a missionary; plus mission-related blogs, podcasts, and videos.

POMnet.org

Support and resources for the parents of missionaries.

Urbana.org > Next Steps > Ask Jack

Gives hundreds of answers to questions on missions as well as on other key global issues.

PRAYER RESOURCES FOR COUNTRIES AND PEOPLES

Global Prayer Digest

Global-prayer-digest.org

Missionary stories, biblical challenges, urgent reports, and exciting descriptions of unreached peoples; devotional; available in monthly booklet or daily e-mail.

Operation World

Patrick Johnstone and Jason Mandryk

OperationWorld.org

Vital information and specific prayer points for each country in the world.

MISSION-RELATED BOOKS

2020 Vision: Amazing Stories of What God Is Doing Around the World

Bill and Amy Stearns (Bethany House)

Exciting breakthroughs in new harvest fields are highlighted, along with scriptural insights into God's heart for the nations and practical ways for individuals and churches to get involved.

Christian Heroes: Then and Now

Janet and Geoff Benge (YWAM)

Easy-to-read series of missionary biographies (thirty books, about two hundred pages each).

Cross-Cultural Connections: Stepping Out and Fitting In Around the World

Duane Elmer (IVP)

Provides a compass for navigating through different cultures—how to avoid pitfalls and cultural faux pas as well as how to make the most of opportunities to build cross-cultural relationships.

CultureShock! A Survival Guide to Customs and Etiquette

(Marshall Cavendish Corporation)

A reference series on the customs and etiquette of various countries and cities.

Friend Raising: Building a Missionary Support Team That Lasts

Betty J. Barnett (YWAM)

A practical and genuine approach to life, ministry, and teamwork in missions.

From Jerusalem to Irian Jaya: A Biographical History of Christian Missions

Ruth A. Tucker (Zondervan)

Understand the life and role of missionaries throughout history through their real-life failures and successes.

Funding Your Ministry: Whether You're Gifted or Not

Scott Morton (NavPress)

Addresses the obstacles of support raising and gives a biblical path for recruiting and maintaining donor support.

Global Mission Handbook: A Guide for Crosscultural Service

Steve Hoke and Bill Taylor (IVP)

A practical guide in preparing for intercultural missions, with resources for spiritual preparation, cross-cultural skills, hands-on missionary training, and key questions to ask in selecting a mission agency.

How to Be a World-Class Christian: Becoming Part of God's Global Kingdom

Paul Borthwick (Authentic)

World-class Christians pray world-focused prayers; live lifestyles of stewardship, sacrifice, and solidarity with the poor; and are committed to both local witness and world evangelization. Designed for individual and group study.

*I Think God Wants Me to Be a Missionary: Issues to Deal with
Long before You Say Goodbye*

> Neil Pirolo (Emmaus Road International)
>
> Helps missionary candidates look closely at scores of issues
> that should be clarified long before they say goodbye.

*Ministering Cross-Culturally: An Incarnational Model for
Personal Relationships*

> Lingenfelter and Mayers (Baker)
>
> A mission classic that examines the significance of the
> Incarnation for effective cross-cultural ministry; the authors
> demonstrate that Jesus needed to learn and understand the
> culture in which he lived before he could undertake his public
> ministry.

On Being a Missionary

> Thomas Hale (William Carey Library)
>
> Drawing on his years of experience as a veteran missionary to
> Nepal, as well as the input of many others, Dr. Hale deals with
> the problems, struggles, and failures missionaries often face.

*Parents of Missionaries: How to Thrive and Stay Connected
When Your Children and Grandchildren Serve Cross-Culturally*

> Cheryl Savageau and Diane Stortz (Authentic)
>
> A counselor's professional insight and a parent's personal
> journey teach parents of missionaries to understand mission-
> ary life, to navigate holidays, to grandparent long-distance,
> and to say goodbye well.

People Raising: A Practical Guide to Raising Support
  William P. Dillion (Moody Press)
  A highly practical guide that gives tools to move beyond building a donor list to sharing a vision and drawing others into a vital ministry team.

Scaling the Wall: Overcoming Obstacles to Missions Involvement
  Kathy Hicks (Authentic)
  Personal stories from missionaries in many organizations about how God overcame their fears and obstacles and met their needs in ways they never could have expected.

Screams in the Desert: Hope and Humor for Women in Cross-Cultural Ministry
  Sue Eenigenburg (William Carey Library)
  Participate in one woman's humorous accounts of life overseas and the lessons she learned along the way. Sue gives poignant insights into issues many women encounter on the mission field.

Serving As Senders: How to Care for Your Missionaries
  Neil Pirolo (Emmaus Road International)
  Learn how to care for missionaries you know while they prepare to go, while they're on the field, and when they return home. You'll be amazed at how active you can be in missions.

Spiritual Warfare for Every Christian: How to Live in Victory and Retake the Land
  Dean Sherman (YWAM)
  A must-read, no-nonsense, "both feet planted on the ground" approach to the unseen world.

Tentmaking: Business as Missions

Patrick Lai (Authentic)

An in-depth reference for existing tentmakers of proven, workable alternatives to conventional missionary life and work overseas; drawn from interviews with 450 people.

Victory Over the Darkness: Realizing the Power of Your Identity in Christ

Neil T. Anderson (Regal)

Based on Christ's promise "You will know the truth, and the truth will make you free," Anderson emphasizes the cardinal truths of Scripture as a base from which to renew our minds and fend off Satan's relentless attempts to convince us that we are less than Christ empowers us to be.

For more mission books and publishers, visit GoConnect. org/booksources and AskAMissionary.com > Books.

MISSION-HELPFUL COURSES

Boot Camp for Personal Support Raising

TheBodyBuilders.net

An intense two-day seminar that trains Christian workers how to get their ministry assignment funded quickly and fully.

Business as Mission

BusinessAsMissionNetwork.com

News, resources, and tools to turn good business into great ministry; extensive source of resources, seminars, conferences, and courses.

Encountering Islam

   Keith Swartley, editor (Authentic)

   EncounteringIslam.org

   A semester-long course on Islam, which gives a working knowledge of the Islamic faith and an understanding of how to share with Muslims the life of Christ.

Experiencing God: Knowing and Doing the Will of God

   Henry Blackaby (B&H Publishing)

   Blackaby.org

   A modern classic on how God is working in the world today and how we can join him in his work (not the other way around).

Missionary Training International

   MTI.org

   Prefield training in the vitals of cross-cultural ministry; prefield program in language acquisition techniques; postfield debriefing and renewal; training for children and teens.

Perspectives on the World Christian Movement

   U.S. Center for World Missions (William Carey Library)

   Perspectives.org

   A fifteeen-lesson course that unfolds God's plan for the world and our roles as individuals and churches. Every prospective missionary should take this course. Classes online and in cities around the world (listed on website).

Tentmaking

   GlobalOpps.org

   Empowering tentmakers to reach the world through resources, events, and training.

World Christian Foundations

U.S. Center for World Missions

USCWM.org > Programs and Publications

Study anywhere in the world with a qualified tutor to get a solid liberal arts education from a mission-oriented perspective.

For comprehensive directories of mission courses, visit GoConnect.org/introtomissions and AskAMissionary.com > Courses.

LINKS TO MISSION INFORMATION

ELS-jobs.com

Database and links to English-teaching opportunities around the world; summer or one-year assignments; volunteer, partial-pay, and support-raised positions available.

GoConnect.org/resources

Annotated links to about anything you could need regarding missions.

MisLinks.org

Exhaustive directory on everything mission, including practical mission, missions by regions of the world, mission topics and information, academic research for missions.

MissionaryResources.org

Assortment of articles, links, books, videos, and discussion forums.

MissionResources.com

Resources from A to Z for missionaries and Christians worldwide.

Mukappa.org

Links to resources, spiritual and social support, and practical assistance for missionary kids.

Oscar.org.uk

Gateway to useful information, advice, and resources for missions and Christian service around the world.

MISSION HELP FOR YOUR CHURCH

ACMC.org

Advancing Churches in Missions Commitment, a network of mission-active churches and organizations through which your church can get practical assistance tailored to your church's global outreach needs.

GoConnect.org/goteam

Directory of mobilization ministries, resources, conferences, consulting, and coaching to help incorporate missions into the life of your church.

GoConnect.org/networking

Links to local and regional mission-training opportunities and services for many U.S. metro areas as well as a growing number of citywide mission-activist networks.

MISSION MAGAZINES AND NEWSLETTERS

Ask A Missionary

AskAMissionary.com > Newsletters

Quarterly e-newsletter on becoming a missionary, with mission-related Q&As, magazines, books, conferences, and Internet sites.

Brigada.org

Weekly e-newsletter announcing upcoming mission events around the world, new resources, and mission courses.

Daily Connections

GoConnect.org/daily

Keep in touch with trends affecting missions in the North American church as well as upcoming mission conferences, events, articles, strategies, and resources; daily e-mail or RSS feed.

Global Prayer Digest

Global-prayer-digest.org

Missionary stories, biblical challenges, urgent reports, and exciting descriptions of unreached peoples; devotional; available in monthly booklet or daily e-mail.

Lausanne World Pulse

LausanneWorldPulse.com

Monthly e-magazine providing mission and evangelism news, events, information, and analysis.

Mission Frontiers

MissionFrontiers.org

Bimonthly postal-mailed magazine dedicated to fostering a global movement to establish an indigenous, self-reproducing, church planting movement among all unreached peoples.

Perspectives in Practice

Perspectives.org > Next Steps > Resource Center

Monthly e-magazine inspires with testimonies, practical tips, and ideas to go, send, pray, welcome, and mobilize for mission as well as information on business-as-mission.

RESOURCES FOR WOMEN IN MISSIONS

Parents of Missionaries: How to Thrive and Stay Connected When Your Children and Grandchildren Serve Cross-Culturally

Cheryl Savageau and Diane Stortz (Authentic)

A counselor's professional insight and a parent's personal journey teach parents of missionaries to understand missionary life, to navigate holidays, to grandparent long-distance, and to say goodbye well.

Peter's Wife

PetersWife.org

Monthly e-newsletter with help and encouragement for missionary wives and moms.

Through Her Eyes: Life and Ministry of Women in the Muslim World

Marti Smith (Authentic)

A candid look from married and single women at issues women face living cross-culturally—loneliness, learning a new language, helping children adjust, maintaining healthy marriages, and balancing ministry and family roles.

True Grit: Women Taking on the World, for God's Sake

Deborah Meroff (Authentic)

Powerful guide to women's issues around the world—honor killings, child brides, female infanticide, and others—told through the stories of nine women who are making a difference.

Women of the Harvest

WomenOfTheHarvest.com

Bimonthly e-newsletter with articles by women who know the difficulties of adjusting to a new culture, stumbling over a new language, and finding a place in ministry.

For more mission titles go to
www.authenticpublishing.com.
You can also sign up to receive "The Missional Mind"
e-newsletter, plus receive a free missions eBook when
you do.

Other Authentic titles to look for:

*OPERATION WORLD: The Definitive Prayer Handbook
for the Nations and Peoples of the World* (updated
August 2010 release) 9781850788621

*HOW TO BE A WORLD CLASS CHRISTIAN: Becoming
Part of God's Global Kingdom* 9781934068342

*WINDOW ON THE WORLD: When We Pray, God
Works* 9781932805918

*DISCOVERING CHURCH PLANTING: An Introduction
to the Whats, Whys, and Hows of Global Church
Planting* 9781606570296

*THE MISSION MINDED FAMILY: Releasing Your
Family to God's Destiny* 9781934068434

*THE MISSION MINDED CHILD: Raising a New
Generation to Fulfill God's Purpose* 9781932805888

*BREAKTHROUGH: The Return of HOPE to the
Middle East* 9781934068632

*IN THE PRESENCE OF THE POOR: Changing the
Face of India* 9781606570128

Available at www.authenticpublishing.com,
(800) 524-1588, or at your favorite online
or local book source.

OPERATION WORLD

THE DEFINITIVE PRAYER HANDBOOK FOR THE NATIONS AND PEOPLES OF THE WORLD

JASON MANDRYK

**Available
August 2010,
the all new and revised
Operation World Book
and CD Rom**

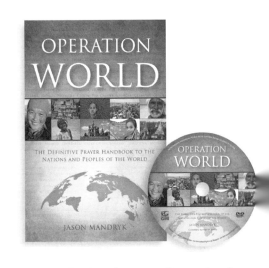

Operation World is the definitive global prayer handbook. With over 1 million copies of past versions being sold, this all new 7th edition has been completely updated and revised by Jason Mandryk and again covers the entire populated world. *Operation World* gives you the information necessary to be a vital part in fulfilling God's passion for the nations.

Included in the updated and revised edition:

- Daily Prayer Calendar
- 221 countries included
- Maps of each country
- Geographic Information
- People Groups within each country
- Economic Information

- Political Information
- Religious make-up of each country
- Answers to Prayer
- Challenges for Prayer
- Persecution index

August 2010 • HB/PB, 832 pages, 6 X 9
HB 9781850788614 • PB 9781850788621 • CD ROM 9781850788744